TEST TUBES
& TROWELS
Using Science in Archaeology

TEST TUBES
& TROWELS
Using Science in Archaeology

Kevin Andrews and Roger Doonan

TEMPUS

For David Turner

First published 2003

Tempus Publishing Ltd
The Mill, Brimscombe Port
Stroud, Gloucestershire GL5 2QG
www.tempus-publishing.com

© Kevin Andrews and Roger Doonan, 2003

The right of Kevin Andrews and Roger Doonan to be identified
as the Authors of this work has been asserted in accordance with
the Copyrights, Designs and Patents Act 1988.

British Library Cataloguing in Publication Data.
A catalogue record for this book is available from the British Library.

ISBN 0 7524 2918 3

Typesetting and origination by Tempus Publishing.
Printed and bound in Great Britain.

CONTENTS

PREFACE

Covering aspects of archaeological science such as artefact analysis, understanding ancient technology, trade and exchange and dating materials, this book critically explores the pace and application of scientific techniques in the discipline of archaeology. Massive advances in archaeological understanding through the appliance of science have been made in areas that were once thought to be irrecoverable. Nevertheless, the application of increasingly sophisticated analytical techniques has often masked poor archaeological questions, or perhaps stated something which can sometimes be obvious to simple non-technical observation. Conversely some aspects of understanding our past which were once thought obvious have been thrown into confusion by revelations borne of changes in archaeological science. This book also explores the complex and often uncomfortable relationship between science, history, anthropology, politics and theory. The use and abuse of science within archaeological understanding are presented through a series of thematic case studies.

Science defined as the systematic study of the nature and behaviour of the material and physical universe based on experiment, measurement, and the formulation of general covering laws – excludes by that definition abstract ideational theory of anything that does not exist. Archaeological interpretation involves the building of representations of how people once lived and behaved through the application of abstract theory. Archaeological interpretation, although rooted in the study of material remains (including the scientific investigation of their physical, chemical and biological characteristics) has to jump across a divide from the material to the ideational. This book is about jumping across that divide.

A clear understanding of how science is used (and misused) within archaeology requires a study of the theory of archaeological knowledge. An investigation of the validity, methods and scope of archaeology will clarify how archaeological knowledge may be built. Such an investigation can also explore how archaeological knowledge might be undermined. This book explores the theoretical backdrop to the study of archaeology and attempts to explain the sometimes capricious relationship between scientific method and archaeological interpretation.

One of our major themes is that there is a gulf of misaligned aims and objectives between archaeometrists (scientists, if you like) and archaeologists (theorists, if you like). As with all introductory texts, we will inevitably make sweeping generalisations and exaggerations. We just made one. Scientists do not operate outside of theory, and some archaeologists see their job as purely technical and leave interpretation to others. Forgive our characterisations, and generalisations, we believe they are a crucial pump to prevent our necessarily small boat being overwhelmed by the swell of literature and debate.

In the past the focus of books concerning archaeological science has been on the various materials encountered by archaeologists, or on the different techniques employed by archaeometrists. As a result there is a tendency for potential readers to be put off by overly technical considerations that lead away from the subject of understanding the lives of past people. Our focus will be on the questions that archaeologists ask where archaeological science can be employed to help resolve those questions. We will concentrate on themes rather than techniques.

The production of this book would not have been possible without the help and support of many colleagues. Prof. Tim Darvill is owed particular thanks for helping to foster an open and inclusive research culture in which colleagues can fully participate in the Billown Project, of which he is director. This has allowed a productive amalgam of training through research which has permeated the learning and teaching culture at Bournemouth University and has encouraged the development of a closer relationship between archaeometry and archaeological practice where scientific methodology and theory are placed at the root of archaeological excavation; we recommend all readers to his current and forthcoming publications. Similarly colleagues and former mentors elsewhere have been invaluable in setting up pathways to research; they include Prof. John Collis and Prof. Barbara Ottaway.

Many others have helped in offering support and advice in ways they are probably unaware of themselves. They include Dr Peter Day for stimulating many points in the text, Dr Miles Russell for quiet calmness, Dr Helen Smith for helping to make our working environment workable and liveable, Dr Ian Whitbread for extended discussions in Athens, Dr Michael Boyd and Dr Chris Cumberpatch for pulling apart accepted norms, Melody Austin for illustrations, and Felix Doonan for inspiration and motivation. In the later stages the organisational and hospitality skills of Marina Miltiadou were outstanding and without her help the final document would never have made it to the publishers. We thank friends and family in Gt. Yarmouth, Coventry, Greece and Cyprus, the students of the University of Bournemouth, and others too numerous to mention. Lastly we thank, David Turner, Theologian, Historian, and East-Romanist, whose historical perversity has been a constant source of joy and who sadly is no longer able to read this book although thankfully he knew it all anyway!

1

UNDERSTANDING THE RELATIONSHIP

What is archaeology and what is archaeological science?

Very few archaeologists attend archaeological science conferences; conversely at conferences organised by archaeologists, there are few archaeometrists (archaeological scientists) to be seen. Why are these groups not more interested in each other's work? What is archaeology, what is archaeological science, and how do they relate to each other? Simple answers to these questions would be: archaeology is the study of the human past through material remains while archaeological science is the use of scientific techniques and experiments to reveal more clues about material remains. This book could give a straightforward account of the whole range of scientific instrumentation available to the archaeologist. Such books, however, have already been written: they tend to present scientific techniques in a hierarchy depending upon their sophistication. Their chapters deal with different materials such as metals, ceramics, lithics and glass. The focus of such texts and their organisation tells us something important about the interface between archaeology and archaeological science. There is a sense of celebration of what archaeological science has achieved so far, spurred on with confident expectation of what technological innovation will bring in the future. The evolution of new instruments with better precision, increased sensitivity and lower detection limits will supposedly allow us to better analyse more materials.

However, we do not share this sense of optimism, instead feeling that the faith placed in new techniques is nothing more than a myth promulgated to support a particular set of flawed ideas about how archaeological science is practised. Some of these issues relate to training/background of individuals that result in the divisions we mentioned above. We find it more interesting to return to the intellectual context within which archaeological science is practiced to explore the nature of the relationship between archaeology and science. This is not to reduce this text to a paradigmatic contemplation; we are eager to discuss techniques and do this through example, illustrating our points with case studies. We hope to demonstrate that the application of science in archaeology will not be improved by having better machines, more funding and bigger laboratories, rather, what is needed is a critical re-evaluation of ideas of what is being studied, and how this impacts on methodology.

Almost all dictionary definitions of archaeology fall into the trap of acknowledging 'the past' as a reality, a definitive string of events. This is simply not the case. The past did not happen. The past, as we try to understand it, is created in the present, this is what writing history is actually about: the weaving together of understandings about people's activities in times and places different to our own. It is a kind of travel writing if you like, addressing a set of impressions about the possible meanings of material remains. With history, the material remains are documentary records. Here it would *seem* that we are on safer ground to insist that the past is a reality. However, as international politics shows us today, we cannot trust the written word to define or describe realities.

We can draw a parallel with history to underline the bizarre nature of the past in the present. Historians write history relative to their own situation and experience at that time, so history is a reflexive and relative subject that boils down to a critical appraisal of the lines of evidence. Historical events, therefore, can be interpreted in a multitude of ways.

The reality of what happened in the past is something that is experienced by individuals and groups in different ways depending on a kaleidoscope of influences from education, social status, political awareness, access to information and the control of information. When people who have experienced an event then write it down, they do so with their own kaleidoscopic twist. Someone else may have a completely different view of the pattern of events that they have witnessed. Years later when we re-read an historical narrative of an event, we do so with our own set of experiences, biases and priorities which colour and twist the pattern of the event yet again. There is never one immutable, unchangeable and definitive reality of what happened in the past, because we create the past now and that interpretation is open to further change through the relative filters of reception and understanding. Particular combinations of historical evidence and strong elements of reception and understanding can become fossilised into 'set piece' landmark events that become accepted wholesale across wider social groups and passed from one generation to the next. The Battle of Hastings, evil King John, the experience of the Industrial Revolution, the excesses of the French Revolution are just some examples of accepted histories which have to be consciously re-examined and deconstructed in order to review the evidence and recreate a past in the present. Of course, history is also political and accompanied by

9

moral and ethical issues. Just as the writing of history is a responsibility that should not be taken lightly, so too is the engagement in archaeological practice.

The flux of historical interpretation has been reflected in archaeological interpretations where accepted ideas have fossilised into 'facts' without us really noticing, in conjunction with the socially constructed (and socially accepted) 'big stories' such as theories of progression and social evolution. Uncritical archaeologists have tended to squeeze evidence into voguish 'big story' moulds to produce the Neolithic farming revolution, the three-age system of techno-logical progression and recognised culture groups such as the 'Celts'. Critical re-examination of some of the widely accepted 'landmark facts' from prehis-tory can show some of them to be the products of socio-political conditioning surrounding their emergence as much as they are representations of archaeo-logical fact. Simon James, for example, has argued strongly that the modern idea of ancient 'Celts' is mainly the product of the nationalistic ambitions of groups in the nineteenth-century interpretation of evidence, rather than a reality from prehistory.

Little wonder that archaeologists working from evidence in the form of material remains of past activities have an even more difficult time with inter-pretation. As archaeologists, we have to use our 'archaeological imagination' (a term first used by Leroi-Gourhan) to bring colour and life to the past but, at the same time, rein in that imagination by hanging our narratives on a credible framework supported by scientific data.

Relating to past times

We find it difficult to relate to the lives of past people, not only because of their absence, but because of the ways in which we are socially, politically and tech-nologically conditioned to live in; vast urban environments that are utterly alien to the ways of life in the remote past. A related point is that we should not fall into the trap of viewing this difference in terms of inevitable trajecto-ries of technological and social evolution. We are not necessarily more complex, more socially and technologically sophisticated than people living in the past; we are simply different. Focusing on the differences and attempting to explain them beyond the obvious explanation of inevitable technological and social progression is one of archaeology's greatest challenges and the area in which archaeological science has committed its greatest crimes. The reason for this is that archaeological science has found itself at home with artefact analysis and accounting for their production. Models of social and technolog-ical progress are hard-wired into our ways of thinking. Practitioners in archae-ological science tend to lack critical self-reflection. This is no surprise if they considered the world to be completely knowable and absolute with a single past; there is simply no room for alternatives.

There is a tendency to view technological progress as an inevitable consequence of our scientific outlook. Within this view, objective scientific method will always unravel the next stage of the progression. Therefore, in time, Faggot torches almost automatically transform through the progression into oil lamps, to candles, to gas lamps and ultimately into electric light bulbs (**1**). What is lost through this hard-wired model of progress is the realisation that technology, far from being isolated from social choice, is central to social action. The ways in which people make choices about how they innovate, produce and consume the things they and others produce is central to social interaction and social reproduction. In other words, technology is a fully social phenomenon.

So what is it that archaeologists and scientists study? Many archaeologists would consider that they study the 'archaeological record', the present material reality of past events and processes. The archaeological record is the thing that we dig up. As we do so, this is translated into an archive or other form of record that supposedly represents the primary record. The archive record is systematically and objectively organised information (or clues) that can be used to make inferences about what that record might mean in terms of past human behaviour and experiences.

The big problem of archaeological inquiry is that we cannot be wholly objective in our observations. Through the process of excavation the subject of inquiry, the record is destroyed. The subject of inquiry is also massive – entire sites or landscapes – and usually under threat from development. Observations have to be made on samples taken from the whole under considerable time restraints. Decisions have to be made as to what is significant and

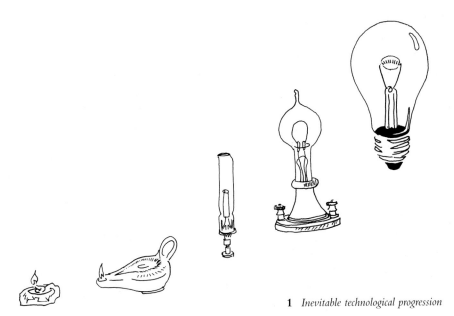

1 *Inevitable technological progression*

what samples should be taken. Decisions are made by individuals with a particular up-bringing and training which inevitably colours the choices made (through subconscious biases and interests, for example). Other subtleties seriously affect the recording process. Features within sites can be missed because of the vagaries of the weather. For example, features such as ditches, post holes and pits may show up clearly one day after a light shower of rain but be missed on another dry day when subtle differences in soil colour are not as evident. The archaeological 'record' is not objectively approachable in a scientific sense of strictly controlled experimentation under uniform conditions.

This fragmentary nature of the record in its formation and recovery has in part led to some archaeologists rejecting the very notion of the record. We are inclined to agree with them. Armed with our archaeological imagination, how can we proceed with a study of human relationships by assuming that the integrity of such study is grounded in the degree to which we can accurately identify their material representation? We should stop and really think about what is being represented in the so-called record. The problem of its being fragmentary and a belief that we have to stay close to it, results in it giving us a very perverse view of humanity. Enter fiction, enter the archaeological imagination, but with a firm hand on the reins. We have to reconsider how our archaeological encounters relate to the dynamic practice of humans, action and the body; this is not fiction but a way of using evidence in a more sensual, locatable manner, not simply placing a false sense of security in fragmentary remains. With these issues concerning the 'archaeological record' in mind what claims of objectivity can science really make? Herein lays the problem of scientific application within archaeology.

David Clarke, a renowned Cambridge scholar and advocate of scientific approaches, summarised the discipline of archaeology as the theory and practice for the recovery of unobservable human behaviour patterns from indirect traces in bad samples. This rather cynical yet honest appraisal of archaeological practice leads us to an understanding of why archaeology uses the natural sciences in its search for evidence. In order to glean the most from bad samples, archaeometrists try to squeeze as much relevant information from their samples. Archaeometry literally means the measurement of old things, a term coined by Christopher Hawkes in 1958. In its early use, archaeometry was usually restricted to the application of the physical and chemical sciences in the service of archaeology, whilst the biological sciences of botany, zoology and ecology were described within the established tradition of environmental archaeology that was also labelled 'archaeological science'. More recently these distinctions have been obscured. Most people now regard 'archaeometry' and 'archaeological science' to embrace all ancient materials and their scientific investigation, as well, of course, as the investigation of modern standards, correlates from experimental archaeology and the products of geological and environmental sampling.

Archaeometry might involve, for example, an estimate of the age of the sample, its chemical make-up or its state of preservation. Microscopic observations can be made that might inform us about matters such as manufacturing techniques (such as metallurgical microstructures) or diseases and traumas (such as microscopic disruptions of tooth growth). Analysis of trace elements or diagnostic inclusions within pottery has the potential to indicate origins of manufacture. Statistical approaches are employed in order to seek out patterns in data and test their significance. Geophysical sciences are employed in order to detect features buried within deposits and to plan excavation campaigns in order to make the most of limited resources. Environmental sciences are used in order to reconstruct the landscapes and climates of the past. In many ways, then, archaeology uses scientific approaches and techniques from the natural sciences, from physics, chemistry and biology. However, archaeology is not in itself a scientific discipline that operates within scientifically provable laws – there are no reliable formulae to define culture or to precisely predict the outcome of an excavation. The questions that archaeologists ask are inherently subjective. Here lies the paradox of archaeology.

We live in a society where the word 'subjective' has attained a vaguely negative connotation, owing to the perceived strength of objective science. The world-view of objective science being a 'good thing', however, has been eroded in the later twentieth century. Matthew Johnson has shown how the work of Francois Lyotard characterised the general distrust of science in the twentieth century as 'the post-modern condition' – a state of knowledge pervading Western capitalist societies. Archaeology too has been through a transformative change in theoretical perspective through the twentieth century. The circle of theory and practice in archaeology has revolved from a position of description and recording of material remains, to explaining them in terms of past human activity, to interpretations of past human experience of living in past worlds. As this circle slowly turned, the many archaeologists involved in the practice of archaeology had different views as to where their interests were situated relative to other disciplines. Some saw archaeological interpretation as a reflexive exercise in writing prehistory that was inevitably pregnant with contemporary political and social influences. These archaeologists viewed archaeology as having close ties to history as a discipline. They saw archaeological evidence as a text to be read and interpreted, the objects and features as symbols of past experiences. Others situated archaeology in line with the sciences, viewing the relative nature of history as anathema to the scientific process. Such archaeologists viewed archaeological remains as static, physical realities – fragments that could be linked to the dynamics of past human behaviour through universal scientific laws developed and tested through the appliance of science.

Archaeology, almost by default and no matter where we position ourselves on the circle of theory and practice, has become obsessed with the objects rather than the people associated with those objects. Some scholars making this point have described this as 'fetished archaeology'. Excavated objects were described and categorised in the antiquarian era of the discipline. Applying theoretical arguments to attempt to explain what may have happened in the past to form the material remains that are available to us for study, was overtly avoided. Indeed, theory was seen by pioneering archaeologists such as Pitt Rivers as an evil to be avoided. Fullness and accuracy of description were the watchwords by which archaeologists developed their discipline. Archaeology has now moved on to regard material remains as a window to interpretation and explanation of a past. In doing so, it has embraced theory following the realisation that description is *not* explanation. Many theoretical bridges have been formed to connect the material remains examined today with the people who lived in the past. Many of them have collapsed under the weight of criticism that they led to unsatisfactory pasts. Other more solid theoretical bridges currently survive. One relatively recent bridge that we believe leads to an exciting and promising past where people are discussed alongside features, artefacts, architecture and the nature of social relations relates to the notion of 'Agency' and will prove to be a recurrent theme in this volume.

Agency is one of those rather nebulous terms with many contributions, some contentious, as to how to best define it (see chapter seven for a fuller account). We can follow social theory to consider how individuals may be *attributed* with agency, in part the act of doing. The focus of analysis therefore becomes the attribution of aspects of technological and social action as read through the material remains of that action. We therefore avoid falling into the trap of replacing one fetish of objects with another hooked on individuals. Instead, we can concentrate on the action of the past. Agency becomes an important concept with which we can more effectively mould our understanding of material remains.

Agency

Material remains can, in part, be regarded as the result of human action. This is not to reduce agency simply to action or doing but rather to elucidate the concept of agency as being rooted in action. Coming to understand what we mean by action in turn helps us to understand agency. Agency is a concept for appreciating how intentions through actions located in time and space recreate the social relations and material reality within which the agents already find themselves entangled. If we are forced to reduce the agent to the individual, then agency must be seen to extend beyond the corporeal reality of that individual through influential gestures and the modification of the physical and social world. Agency is scrutinised in an arena accompanied by concepts of time, space and historical and material contingency. By this we mean that action weaves together time and space but the reality of that action is impacted upon by constraints of the material world (material contingency) and by the expectations of the actor and others around by virtue of their memory and understanding of tradition (historical contingency). Acknowledging the interdependence of these elements within a single arena of scrutiny should allow the reader to understand the thematic organisation of the chapters in this book. Although each case study could address any of these issues, different ones are emphasised in turn to illustrate the point.

To achieve a useful interpretation of the material remains in terms of human behaviour, we must place the event in space and time. This involves dating the material remains and mapping them into a context relative to other known remains. It also involves relating them to other sets of material. Are they isolated or grouped? Have they been moved from where they were originally deposited? How have they been moved? All these questions are important in placing the remains within an archaeological context that is the stage for action. How might our interpretations change if we could see the remains set in a deliberate clearing within a wooded environment, as opposed to a swampy overgrown location? Material remains may reflect the choices that people make. It is understanding how agents negotiate alternatives in the face of practical and social realities that is of interest to the archaeologist. Cleary, such methodological requirements are wide open for the application of scientific means of enquiry; it is a pity that they have rarely been applied within such a theoretical context.

The scope and history of archaeological science

Excavating, analyzing and interpreting buried objects, structures and remnants that give clues to the lives of past people and *how* they lived their lives is one of the most interesting intellectual pursuits for those of us interested in human beings. Its recent popularity is attested by the explosion of attention given over to archaeological interests in the media, especially television. Archaeology, as a discipline, has many faces, it is many things to many people. Archaeology can be seen as educational providing a whole series of insights into central questions. Recently Clive Gamble outlined these central questions in his book *Archaeology the Basics* as being the unravelling of the stories of: human evolution; the beginning of farming; the origins of modernity; the origins of urban life and human civilisation; the phenomenon of global colonisation of the human race. Thus archaeology can help to satisfy an inherent interest in our past.

Archaeology can also be seen as functional, whereby many societies have placed institutionalised values on archaeological remains that are sometimes protected. In relation to building and development of today's roads, cinema and shopping complexes, housing and utility networks, archaeology has a necessary function of investigating remains to allow decisions to be made about their recording, preservation or destruction. Archaeology has attached to it a range of legal and illegal pursuits relating to the investigation and conservation of sites and monuments.

For others archaeology may be a form of entertainment, a source of inspiration for games, films or television. For others, archaeology may be a source of contention as results of investigation are used to refute or legitimate competing claims to political power or formation or destruction of national or ethnic identities. The cultural remains of the past can also be a source of controversy where they have been obtained illegally and held by museums outside of the present-day group claiming them as part of their own national heritage. Black market forces have penetrated archaeology whereby today more money exchanges hands for illegally gained antiquities than for certain restricted drugs. Archaeological science has long been involved in the authentication of illicit antiquities for the art market. These are just some of the faces of archaeology. If we attach descriptors to archaeology, therefore, there are many that fit depending on the form of interaction one has with the discipline. Archaeology can be profitable, necessary, a waste of time, inspirational, boring, entertaining, political, puzzling, fascinating, and frustrating. Equally it is a professional practice, a hobby and an academic pursuit; technical, theoretical, artistic and scientific.

From the 1950s, university and museum departments rapidly established scientific research laboratory facilities that focused on art history and archaeological materials, for example the Research Laboratory for Archaeology and the History of Art at Oxford. The first bulletin of this laboratory was published in 1958, later to develop into the journal *Archaeometry*. Studies began to be differentiated under the umbrella term of 'archaeometry' into distinct areas of interest. By the 1960s, interest in the botanical and zoological applications of earth sciences to investigate the environmental aspects of archaeological data emerged as a distinct constituency of 'environmental archaeologists'. In 1961 the first comprehensive overview of the development of archaeometry, *Science in Archaeology: A Survey of Progress and Research* by Don Brothwell and Eric Higgs, was published. By the mid-1970s professorial positions were established in university departments, together with further specialist journals such as the *Journal of Archaeological Sciences* (first published in 1974).

Thomas Kuhn maintained that advances in scientific knowledge progressed courtesy of enlightening bursts of genius and insights that come as complete revelations to those working within a discipline. Kuhn argued this is because it is impossible to see beyond the current paradigm until the moment it is shifted and the old paradigm collapsed. Can we find examples of paradigm 'shifts' in archaeology or, at least, major readjustments to interpretative frameworks? Well, there are some worthy candidates: the development of carbon-14 dating and subsequent collapse of the European prehistoric time frame and related models of diffusion theory represents a major realignment of ideas that had far reaching repercussions in archaeological practice and interpretation. Although the C-14 'revolution' is often presented as a triumph for archaeological science over humanities-based archaeology, it should be noted that in the post-war milieu and with philosophical movements towards ethics, there was already a growing dissatisfaction with cultural-history approaches from within archaeology. It was probably this ground swell of reaction against approaches that seemed to support much of Nazi propaganda that welcomed in the promise of objectivity that C-14 heralded.

Other examples are related to new archaeological discoveries and our developing abilities to scientifically investigate them. Chauvet Cave in France, for example, discovered in 1994, revealed amazing cave art. These were dated using AMS technologies by carbon-14 dating and determined at 32,000 years old, almost twice the age of similarly painted caves elsewhere. The ice mummy, discovered in 1991 in Italy, was perhaps the archaeological find of the twentieth century in terms of the range of material remains including a complete set of composite personal items of organic and inorganic construction preserved *in situ* with a naturally mummified corpse dating back to the Neolithic. Typically, human remains from this era are preserved only through the cultural filters and distortions of funerary ritual and, usually, only inorganic materials such as stone survive. The big surprise was that this Stone Age *man*, with no evidence of a penis, was carrying a copper axe as part of *his* toolkit. A further surprise emerged through the application of computer tomography techniques that revealed that this *man* had died probably as the result of blood loss from an arrow that had been shot into *his* back, the stone point of which remained lodged under *his* shoulder blade. The Stone Age thus became one in which metals were known and the assumed peace and tranquillity of the early farming communities was brought into question.

Oxygen isotope studies have also revolutionised our understanding of the climatic backdrop to the human story. Through geomorphology, the study of the physical features of the surface of the earth and their relationship to its geological structures, it had been determined that there had been at least four major ice ages or glaciations during the Pleistocene in Europe. The problem geomorphologists faced here is that the action of glaciers growing and shrinking effectively wipes out the evidence of previous glacial episodes on the landscape surface. Oxygen isotope determination allows a detailed picture of climatic conditions to be revealed. These details are locked in ice-core characteristics, in particular the oxygen isotope ratio of O-16:O-18 in the frozen water. During an ice age the ratio is affected by the preferential precipitation in snow and ice formation of the lighter isotope. These studies have revealed at least seventeen glaciations instead of four. Other significant advances in archaeometric analysis include the development of gas chronometric analysis of food residues preserved in pottery that enhance subsistence studies and the development of DNA research that allows us to question the relatedness of various groups both in the past and present.

It has often been commented that archaeology as a discipline borrows ideas and techniques from other fields of study and, moreover, that it is inevitably lagging behind those disciplines picking over the remains of collapsed paradigms and techniques. As such, archaeology rolls along with so many constituencies of interest groups that consensus of paradigm definition (let alone shift) is difficult to reach. Since it is possible to hold so many conflicting interpretations based on archaeological evidence, the idea of revolutionary bursts of pan, disciplinary genius is difficult to imagine.

Archaeological science and archaeological theory

Through the scientification of archaeology, new techniques and interpretations promised to revolutionise our study of the past. A 'new' archaeology emerged during the growth of archaeological sciences during the late 1960s and 1970s which set out to break-down human behaviour into subsystems, to focus on the *processes* through which people lived and to generate law-like, scientifically robust statements about human behaviour. Methodologically, the processual approach enhanced archaeological practice immeasurably. In terms of inter-pretation, however, after decades of research and critical reaction, it has been realised that the previously dominant culture-history approach had irreplace-able qualities that were lost when processual agendas began to dominate the discipline. Principle amongst these qualities was the ability of the culture-historical approach to imagine the detail of people in the past. Culture-historical approach invests in the people of the past, through interpretation, the quality of living, making choices and, in short, being human with the entire historical and cultural colour that animates such a past. This approach served to particularise archaeology and see each set of data within its own context (contextual archaeology). The processual approach saw such context and colours as a cultural smoke-screen that obscured scientific laws of human behaviour. In blowing away the smoke to get at the processual or generalised reasons for behaviour, new archaeology reduced the people of the past into robotic borg-like beings that simply reacted in law-like predictable ways to given circumstances that were usually traced back to aspects of their environ-ments (environmental determinism).

In the later twentieth century archaeologists, especially in Europe, realised that a symbiosis was needed between the methodological advances that were offered by scientific techniques and the interpretative excitement that could be derived from culture-historical approaches. A series of approaches have emerged that have loosely been labelled 'post-processual'. Agency, as a mainstream tenet of such approaches drawn from social theory, aims to reveal the choices and attributes of past actions. In short, archaeologists' interests have largely turned back to the contexts and colours of the past because it has become apparent that, when this is regarded as a smoke screen and blown away, there is nothing left behind it. Human beings cannot be reduced to a set of general laws.

Archaeology appears to many to be in conflict with itself. It appears to be populated by people who simply cannot make up their minds and arrive at definitive truths. Moreover, the ideas of archaeologists, their interpretations of what life was like in the remote past seem, over time, to go round and round in circles. This is seen most clearly in the debate over whether hominids in the early development of the human species were effective hunters, or not. Yes, they were (1960s) . . . perhaps they were not, they may even have been the hunted (1970s), they were definitely very effective hunters (1980s), now we're not too sure one way or the other (1990s) . . . The same can be said of the so-called Neanderthal debate where generations of interpretations have swung from Neanderthals being utterly inhuman in their behaviour, stooped bestial savages, through to them being rather attractive specimens engaging with modern humans and interbreeding with them. Of course what is really happening with the circular interpretations of archaeology is not an inability to reveal definitive truths in time-honoured scientifically verifiable ways by generations of pretty weak and useless archaeologists, but a circulation of inter-pretations that reflect the social, political, economic and cultural milieu from which they emerged. That is why archaeology is such an interesting phenom-enon to engage with and also why it is non-scientific and incapable of producing paradigmatic revelations but will, instead, continually spin around the axis of explanation producing evermore interesting kaleidoscopic patterns of interpretation with which we can do so many exiting things. Archaeology, in short, is rhetoric.

Archaeology as rhetoric

To state that archaeology is an exercise in rhetoric sounds like a dismissal of archaeology's importance. The reason it *sounds* that way is intimately related to our modern condemnation of rhetoric and our preference for objectively defined, scientifically determined arguments. Rhetoric is a stained word. In ancient Greece rhetoric, the art of effective or persuasive speaking or writing, was the foundation of, and root to, quality in thought, philosophy and ulti-mately of life. It also became associated with teachers of rhetoric, the Sophists, who realised that there was political gain to be had in teaching rhetoric. Later this was abused in order that outwardly weaker arguments could usurp stronger arguments.

Those seeking to redress the balance and introduce objective measures by which arguments could be assessed and through which science was progressed, cut off the root to quality. Socrates, Plato and Aristotle, amongst others, began the philosophical and scientific world view that ultimately grew to dominate the Western world. This view championed science as a root to absolute truths and denigrated the use of sophistry and rhetoric. Most people raised in the Western world therefore are conditioned to subconsciously avoid rhetorical arguments and favour a scientific explanation. A key theme to Sophist arguments was that of relativism, the idea that knowledge, morality and other aspects of life are not absolute and therefore absolute truths are impossible. Rhetoric is a vehicle for teaching and understanding quality, the art of seeking out the best argument by means of its virtue. A virtuous argument, of course, is relative to circumstance. The Sophists, therefore, stood for quality through rhetoric.

To overcome the relativism of the Sophists, Plato tried to tie quality down to a fixed concept of good that was subordinate to immutable truth. The struggle, therefore, became one of good (quality) and truth. Aristotle's work came to dominate later medieval philosophy and exerted massive influence on Western scientific tradition. The re-emergence of classical knowledge in the Renaissance became associated with scientific progress, the ultimate conquest of ignorance and triumph over the superstitions of the so-called Dark Ages. Scientific fact and experimentation in quest of 'the truth' came to dominate over relativist quests for quality explanations. Dialectics, the logical investigation of truth, won out over rhetoric. Post-modernist literature often uses the destruction of quality concepts and the advent and adoption of the all-pervasive truth, and the technological world which sprang from it with no understanding of quality to temper it, as a theme.

We have explored a little of the philosophical background to modern ideas about knowledge, science, dialectic and rhetoric, and of our present attitude towards these ideas as a way into a better understanding of what archaeology *should* be about. More importantly, we can use this background to explore what archaeological science *should* be about.

Archaeology as rhetoric underlines the idea that archaeological explanation is about finding the quality explanation using as many lines of data and arguments as needed. Noam Chomsky, the famous linguist, once said: 'As soon as questions of will or decision or reason or choice of action arise, human science is at a loss.' Archaeology is primarily about investigating human choice and human action in the past and, whilst our clues and our data may be obtained by the appliance of science, the various explanations must be argued through to the quality interpretation that is relative to the status of the knowledge base. As more information becomes available, that interpretation may not be the best quality explanation, another will take its place. Archaeology is therefore rhetorical in the best, most virtuous sense. This may be frustrating to many who adhere to the quest for the truth and for scientific explanations of the past; however, for many others the rhetorical nature of archaeology is what makes it such a fascinating and fantastic quest.

Another adjective that aptly describes what archaeology is about is 'eristic', again a word that has vaguely negative connotations. Eristic describes the state of being characterised by disputation, that aims at winning rather than reaching the truth. However, if there is no truth to reach, no single overarching explanation to aim for, but rather, from our rhetorical view of archaeology, a quality interpretation to be wrangled from alternatives, then archaeology is about dispute and persuasion. In order to pursue quality arguments, archaeologists use a battery of techniques, many lines of material evidence and theoretical insights. A problem that has dogged the philosophical position of the post-processualists has been the readiness for detractors to see them as crusaders for relativism and anti-science. A position that views the past as a post-modern playground of endless possible interpretations, that embraces the role of so-called 'fringe' elements such as aliens, mystical forces and new age wierdery in shaping multiple pasts, is a position that has been largely manufactured by the media. The association of post-processual approaches to explaining the past with relativism and 'anything-goes' explanations of the past, however, is part of the polarisation of theoretical positions that does not reflect the aspirations of the vast majority of archaeologists.

Through the lulls in the philosophical arguments, when push comes to shove, most archaeologists of any philosophical position would probably admit that they consider themselves to be investigators trying to find out what happened in the past. It is simply a fact that there are many different ways of investigation and different viewpoints on the quality of resulting interpretations.

The 'conflict' of science and art

Anyone with a thorough grounding in scientific method and trained in rationalist disciplines may well regard the above suggestion that archaeology can be regarded as a rhetorical discipline as insufferably complacent. It is not our intention to alienate either side of the polarised debate that has in recent years affected the wider relationship between scientists and theorists. What we do want to do is to explore the relationship between science and theory as it relates to archaeological practice, as both are essential to it. In order to do this, we need to examine the recent problems that have forced the poles of science and art further apart. These problems are complex, involving large-scale social, political and economic aspects not least governmental funding strategies for example. Inevitably we will need to distil some of the debate and characterise it, perhaps unfairly, in order to plug it into the current investigation of how science and art have managed to form very powerful alliances to investigate a past. Nevertheless, there have been very clear signals that the productive relationship forged between archaeometrists and archaeologists is sometimes an uneasy one. In their summing up of the relevance of archaeo-logical science to archaeology, for example, Pollard and Heron are concerned by generally negative attitudes of some mainstream archaeologists to archaeometry and especially the title of Dunnell's book review: *Why archaeol-ogists don't care about archaeometry*. Others have characterised archaeometry as either peripheral to archaeological interests, or as simply boring. The possible reasons for these characterisations include the lack of integration of scientific applications into theoretically informed and archaeologically relevant questions. Richard Bradley pointed out, that archaeologists criticising archae-ological scientists for investigating problems that contribute little to the core of archaeology can be unfair, especially if they do not communicate what it is they really want to know where science can help provide answers. Mark Pollard and Carl Heron also point out that not all archaeometric research is necessarily focused on archaeological goals but has wider objectives including geological, astronomical, climatological and materials science goals. Michael Tite, a leading figure in the development of archaeometry in Britain, has commented on the need to ensure that the development of new archaeo-metric method is keyed into the provision of data that has real archaeological relevance and that they are not merely expensive new 'toys' looking for a problem to solve.

Another reason for the sometimes mildly antagonistic relationship between archaeometry and archaeology may lie with the divergent intellectual training of the communities involved. Archaeology in Britain has traditionally been placed as an historical humanity, removed from the faculties of pure and applied sciences. Archaeometrists, however, are in the majority scientists who have crossed over in their interests to examine ancient materials. These distanced academic backgrounds have, perhaps unintentionally, created intel-lectual barriers to a fuller integration of the aims and objectives of central interest, which would lead to a more satisfying past.

One of the notable features of archaeological discourse in recent decades has been the involvement of many theoretical approaches of modern European thinkers that have been labelled 'post-modern' and the translation of their ways of thinking into areas of archaeological interpretation. Among these are: Martin Heidegger, Michel Foucault, Pierre Bourdieu, Maurice Merleau-Ponty, Jean Baudrillard, Jacques Derrida, Paul Feyerabend, Karl Popper, Jurgen Habermas and Jean Lyotard. These thinkers have engaged with a great many ideas that have rightly or wrongly been interpreted as an attack or, at least, an erosion of modern science. The characterisation of the sciences and the humanities as being populated by people with completely different outlooks and ways of knowing the world, that are largely incompatible, has been a long-standing one that was perhaps best summarised by the now widespread use of the expression 'the two cultures' popularised by C.P. Snow in 1959. Snow had characterised intellectuals in the humanities as natural Luddites, incapable of appreciating science and, conversely, scientists as a second academic culture that was incapable of appreciating the artistic contexts of the human world outside their laboratories.

When we consider the discipline of archaeology, we can recognise the positions in this polarised debate with archaeologists, trained in humanities traditions, at one end of the field and archaeological scientists, largely trained in positivist traditions, at the other, with the middle ground, where we believe the quality interpretations could be best cultivated, poorly lit and certainly not tended enough by either side.

The debate as to whether archaeology is a subjective exercise in understanding past people, or a hard science capable of determining universal laws of human behaviour ultimately turned out to be an unproductive distraction. Archaeology was too busy in the late 1970s and 1980s arguing about what it was that it allowed itself to be side-lined and hijacked by other agendas. Moreover, the appliance of science in archaeometric research became confused with processual approaches – they are not the same thing. As a result, the various funding structures also became muddled. Novelty of technique was favoured over the quality of application to real archaeological questions. For Rick Jones, addressing a conference on the applications of scientific techniques to archaeology in 1987, some of the most disappointing work in archaeological science was to be found in the field of analysis. Here above all, he maintained, it was possible to argue that you had worthwhile results simply because you had demonstrated that an artefact was made of something. Resources were eaten up on expensive projects of questionable worth, as academics argued over which of the schools of thought offered the best insights into the past. At the same time, professional archaeology was slowly but surely being integrated into the legal and organisational frameworks that privileged the concerns of planners and developers rather than the aims and objectives of the interested fields of research. As a result, archaeology in Britain now has some of the most highly qualified manual labour force of any industry and, at the same time, the most undervalued in terms of reward and career prospects. To add insult to injury, some of the archaeometrists practising in the sterile laboratories work in relatively luxurious conditions with good funding. It is time to recognise that those working in the proximity of the spaces where humans once acted out their social lives are in fact those who should be most valued.

The archaeological endeavour in Britain is becoming evermore fragmented as the organisational and legal frameworks that emerged to fund and protect archaeological deposits became institutionalised and subjected to market forces. The optimistic face of archaeology and its healthy relationship to the media has effectively hid these less successful aspects of the profession. In Britain archaeology has attained a popular image as an absorbing but non-essential pastime creating interest because of the subject matter but equally because of the colourful characters that inhabit archaeology's massive media presence.

The real worth of archaeology as a barometer of past and present social and political values and as the only discipline that can realise the time-depth necessary to resolve some of the most pressing of the planet's problems has not yet been fully appreciated.

The path ahead

In this introductory chapter we have put the appliance of science in archaeology into a disciplinary context. We have moved away from an objects-based approach most often used in outlining archaeological science dividing archaeometry into analyses of various materials such as ceramics, metals, lithics and bone. We offer a programmatic approach that attempts to provide, through thematic case studies, an account of the valuable symbiosis of archaeometric technique within archaeological practice. We arbitrarily align with a theme in each of the following chapters, some harking back to processual interests but, in essence, each chapter looks at a field of analysis caught up within that theme which are aspects relevant to the theoretical position we have outlined above.

Central to this mission is the desire to be explicit about how theoretical concerns directly impact on methodological ones. Pertinent to the thematic approach is our view that analytical investigation in archaeology is an essential, but small part of the overall discipline that needs to be critically appraised in terms of methodology as well as data in order for the results of scientific analysis to be useful to our quest of telling enlightening stories about how people lived in times past.

Within the case studies there are recurrent themes that argue for the critical use of scientific techniques in archaeology that acknowledges the theoretical primacy of investigating the technical choices made by people in the past. The way people did things and the choices people made can reveal much about them and the social, political, economic and ideational aspects of their lives. Crucially, our competing interpretations, debates, controversies and methodologies can reveal to us even more about ourselves and our relationships to the various pasts that we choose to see.

2

IDENTITY
AND POWER

What do we mean by power?

Archaeology can seem a bewildering process. Viewers of television archaeology will be familiar with a range of archaeological practices from geophysics,
landscape survey, excavation, post-excavation artefact examination and the
battery of scientific analyses. How are all these activities brought together in a
single coherent picture? There is no simple answer to this and archaeologists
will probably give varying answers. However, there is no way of disengaging
any part of archaeology from the fact that it tries to develop an understanding
of past human practices. What we want to create are stories about the possibilities of being human in different places and times.

Archaeologists explore how humans behaved by examining the fragmentary
remains of past activities. On the surface it seems uncomplicated. Working out
how somebody made a pot is straightforward, especially with scientific means
of investigation. It is simple to ask: how was this pot made? A *ceramic petrographer* could cut a slither of pot, stick it to a microscope slide and grind it down
until it is so thin that light can pass through it (*thin section analysis*) (**2**). Once
transparent it can be placed under a microscope to determine the orientation
of the inclusions within the sherd. This gives clues as to whether the pot was
hand made or wheel thrown, valuable information about differences in manufacturing techniques that allow us to develop ideas about cultural variation (see
chapter four) or technological choice (see chapter seven). Although the
question 'How was this pot made?' can be answered with the response 'It was
wheel thrown' or 'By hand', such answers are trivial dealing solely with the
technical aspects of how that pot was made. The reality of the pot being made,
though, probably depended on other factors that are far more interesting to the

Thin section petrography

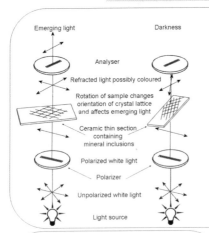

Emerging light — Darkness

Analyser

Refracted light possibly coloured

Rotation of sample changes orientation of crystal lattice and affects emerging light

Ceramic thin section containing mineral inclusions

Polarized white light

Polarizer

Unpolarized white light

Light source

Technique

Thin section petrography uses a polarising microscope. Samples need to be thin enough to transmit light. Plane polarised light is refracted by crystal lattices causing interference. This results in different coloured light emerging or the absence of light. Ceramic petrographers use their knowledge of crystallography and recognition of these effects to identify minerals. As well as mineral identification, recognising mineral orientation, matrix variation and other textural features gives insights into technological choices of the potter.

Sampling

Samples should have at least 1cm^2 available for analysis. Hard samples are prepared by cutting with a diamond saw whilst friable samples, e.g. soils, should be first impregnated with epoxy resin. A flat surface is then prepared and the sample affixed to a glass slide using a suitable adhesive. The sample is then polished down to approximately 30microns.

Finally the section should either be cover slipped with a thin glass slide or polished with ¼ micron paste. Glass cover slips offer the advantage of protecting the sample whilst polishing allows the sample to be examined by other instruments, i.e SEM-EDS, in instances where mineral identification proves difficult.

Cutting a ceramic thin section

Applications

Thin section petrography can be used for any crystalline or composite material that allows the transmission of light. It is used routinely for the characterisation of rocks, ceramics and slags. It is also useful when applied to biological materials such as teeth and bone. It is regularly used in Archaeology for ceramic provenance and technology studies.

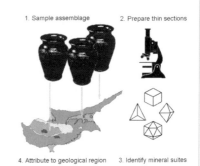

1. Sample assemblage   2. Prepare thin sections

4. Attribute to geological region   3. Identify mineral suites

archaeologist. The making of our pot depends on how the potter managed to acquire their clay: did they own land with a clay deposit or was all clay considered a communal resource? How did the potter manage to spend time making a pot? How did they accumulate the skills to work clay? Why was it desirable to make pots? How was labour organised? How did the potter experience the making of that pot? It seems that a very simple question that can be answered solely in relation to the technical, actually requires the archaeologist to look at bigger issues that reside at the heart of society and individual practice. Asking such questions makes archaeology a fantastic project to be involved in, impacting on how we view our own social institutions and ourselves. Archaeology should court controversy as it unpicks the values that we hold in our own society, which we justify and excuse as 'common-sense'.

There is something central to all human interactions that affect their nature – power. In the everyday-sense, we associate power with energy, the ability to do something. We tend to conceptualise it as something forceful, coercive, compelling, and irresistible. Archaeologists ask questions about power in terms of how groups or individuals acquire power over others, how do some maintain power? Power is a rather nebulous term. Archaeologists seem to use it as a catch-all phrase, like the word 'ritual', as a shortcut to explaining change that they do not fully understand. This has led to fuzzy terms such as 'a shift in power' or 'access to power'. Such terms give the impression that power is something that resides somewhere, you either 'have it' or you don't. Power is not tangible in the physical world, it is not something that can be located in space but it is associated with how we interact with others in light of their status, identity, position and beliefs. Status and identity are made concrete by 'powerful' individuals differentiating themselves with material goods, occupying specific locations at specific times, acting or speaking in certain ways. Most social interactions orbit around accepted rules. This is not to say that there is no tension within interactions. Acknowledging tension in social interaction is an important point because it makes explicit that the outcome of interactions is never predetermined but negotiated. We are agents with free will, not social automata.

So where does this leave us with understanding how archaeologists use the term power? It is probably not wise to ask what power is. We can certainly say what power is not. It is not located in artefacts, places or people but, rather, it is both a stimulus for, and outcome of, social interactions that constitute the richness of social life. What we can say for sure is that it is how power is negotiated in these interactions that in part determine status, identity and practice. It is for these reasons that power is rarely discussed without reference to terms such as identity and status. Let us agree, for the time being, that power is the ability to do things affected by the way agents act. The totality of what people do, the entirety of their social interactions, is a huge remit for archaeologists to study but it is in these interactions that power flows through society. One of the most important stories that archaeologists can attempt to tell is how power is negotiated through social interaction in different societies. What we want to discover is how agents have employed artefacts, spaces, knowledge, memories, expectations and themselves in their negotiation of power.

Social characterisation

If power is the outcome of social interaction, then societies that differ in the way individuals interact, differ too in the way power is articulated. We can therefore use the concept of power to characterise different human groups. We can begin to investigate power by looking at the possibilities of interaction, how people use space, how the material world is brought to bear on social proceedings. Questions can be asked about how distinctions are made within and between groups in terms of how they could act. For instance, if power was articulated in a very uneven manner then it might be that different groups within that society act in quite different ways, whereas a society with a more even power distribution may have less distinction. These are hypothetical generalisations and real human groups have a fascinating tendency to obscure, expose and invert power relations in amazing ways – it pays not to generalise with abstract models but rather just get stuck into investigating the real humanness of society.

Nevertheless, there exists a whole lexicon with which to describe different kinds of human groups. The basis for categorising human groups is invariably how power is articulated within that group. Although not currently popular, there is nothing wrong with characterising societies. However, it is always worth remembering that it is a means of description not explanation. This is a really important point to emphasise since archaeologists have a tendency towards incessant characterisation while not explaining anything. What follows is an introduction to a few terms we use to characterise social groups or polities. By polity we simply mean a politically independent or autonomous social unit. Also the types of interactions associated with each form of polity are reviewed. The classification followed here was devised by an American anthropologist, Elman Service, and has proved to be an enduring system for many archaeologists.

The smallest social unit is termed a band, a social group which numbers less than one hundred, is egalitarian with informal leadership, often mobile as in hunter-gatherer communities with temporary settlements and 'shamans' tending to religious matters. A segmentary society (or tribe) is one which numbers up to one thousand, and exhibits associations with other similar groups. In terms of subsistence such groups tend to be settled farmers along with pastoral farmers who live in permanent villages. Elders control religious matters with calendrical rituals being common. It is common to find specialised architecture which relates to burial, cult practices in dedicated shrines and permanent dwellings.

A term commonly used in the British Iron Age is that of chiefdom. Chiefdom refers to any polity which numbers five thousand to perhaps more than twenty thousand. Ranking and kin-relations are important elements in chiefdoms, which means that many social interactions are determined by an individual's status. It is common in such societies to propose a high-ranking warrior class and a degree of craft specialisation. Unlike bands and tribes, chiefdoms tend to restrict interaction by rank, hence power is articulated in a very different way. Whereas bands may be considered egalitarian with minimal differentiation in the interactions of individuals, chiefdoms are characterised by strict codes on what is appropriate in terms of interaction among individuals of different status. In terms of economic organisation, it is common that commodities are centrally accumulated then redistributed.

Today we are overly familiar with the term state but how is it used archae-ologically? A state comprises in excess of twenty thousand people with a well-defined class-based hierarchy, often under a monarch or emperor. The presence of professional armies is ubiquitous. All the trappings of a modern state are present such as taxation, a defined legal system and a centralised bureaucracy. The landscape is inter-cut with roads linking urban centres with frontier defences and agriculturally productive communities in rural settings. Religious matters are dealt with by a specialised-priest class with monumental temples and places of public worship built alongside palaces and other public buildings. Often the concept of citizen is ingrained in the constitution of that society. Familiar societies such as ancient Greece and Rome would be defined as states.

It is vital to remember that these terms do not explain how power has been negotiated; they merely describe the effect of those negotiations. As mentioned earlier, archaeologists often mistake describing for explaining, forgetting that they are two very different processes. Description tends to be technical and rather boring, explanation is far more fascinating. Explanations often stimulate more interest and debate than a description. One problem that scientific studies have always had is that scientific analyses are really powerful ways of describing things but they rarely explain anything!

One final issue worth noting is how archaeologists approach questions relating to social characterisation. There are basically two different ways of approaching this: one is commonly referred to as the 'bottom-up' approach and the other 'top-down'. Simply put, when trying to characterise polities, we can start with individual practices and actions and how they are performed at the local level; the so-called bottom-up approach. The top-down approach would tend to deal with questions of settlement distribution and trade and exchange patterns first. Although there are times and places that each approach may be more appropriate, it is a theme of this book that most investigations should emphasise the bottom-up approach. The reasons for this are simple yet have huge implications for the way we conceive past societies and for our ethical or political values concerning other human beings both then and now. The difference in these approaches can really be polarised to whether we think that we make society or society makes us. Although many theorists and philosophers have debated this for decades there are some important points to recognise. Firstly, every time we act or do something we reproduce the very society that some would say created us. Therefore, on one hand we do indeed create the society we live within, although clearly we do not do this single-handedly. We also need to acknowledge that everything is to some degree influenced by the social values that we hold close to us in order to allow us to go on with everyday life. Archaeologists have termed this relationship structure and agency. We would argue that society does not recreate itself; rather it is the actions of knowledgeable agents who do this. So in the first instance of archaeological enquiry it would seem sensible to attempt to understand how these agents acted, what were the possibilities of how space was occupied, how were artefacts made and employed? When an attempt has been made understand the local, it is then possible to start trying to understand the regional. As this process of understanding unfolds, initial understandings will invariably be revised.

The problem of scale

Earlier we mentioned how the study of individual inhabitation of space was important to the understanding of social interaction and the need to think about the scale at which archaeologists work to reconstruct the past.

If approaching our investigation from a top-down perspective, we might start looking at settlement patterns, how centres of habitation or practice are located in the landscape. We might employ aerial photographs, landscape survey and field walking to understand the density of sites in a particular location. Such an approach might well have its place but it does not focus on human practice or interaction. The main problem then with a study that works at this macro-scale is that human action is rendered invisible. Our past becomes one of settlement distribution, or territories and resource exchange (see chapter five), an uninhabited past. Since archaeology is, or should be, the study of the human past, then abstracting our past to anything but human practice seems illogical; it seems better to begin at the human scale.

One great thing about field archaeology, be it excavation or landscape studies, is that it gives the investigator the opportunity to inhabit the spaces that other people did hundreds or thousands of years ago. This is a privileged position archaeologists frequently forget. Imagine standing where somebody did thousands of years ago – it is really quiet a special opportunity. Because we have not changed much as a species in terms of our physiology it means that we can use our body as an analytical unit to explore how space was occupied. We can begin to ask what were the possibilities within the space, in light of being in possession of a body. True, what we are thinking, feeling, the cultural values we hold, might be radically different but what we can actually do with ourselves is probably quite similar.

If we stop to pause here, we might begin to realise something that is particularly useful to how we see others and ourselves. We are all used to referring to ourselves as human beings, yet, how often do we ever interact with somebody else's being? If we think of being as all things cerebral, that is thoughts, ideas, feelings and values, then we might realise just how opaque human beings are. We never truly know others' thoughts or feelings, let alone the constructed values they hold. When we interact with other humans it is their doings that we are really witnessing. The being may well inspire these doings but it is the doings that we are really engaging with. At one level, the concept of the human being is not particularly useful to archaeologists to study, much better in some ways to accept and deal with human doings.

Thus investigations at the human scale can be understood in terms of exploring where it is possible and not possible to move, for instance, entrances and exits in structures are ideal for this sort of study. Working at the human scale forces us to think in terms of what the potential is of doing human things within the spaces we occupy. Such approaches are equally at home within domestic or technological structures as they are in ritual landscapes. We can begin to ask questions like 'how was architecture or access to artefacts used to emphasise certain individuals or groups at the expense of others?' In short, analysis at the human scale directly addresses issues of interaction and hence how power is articulated within that polity.

We saw earlier that working at the macro-scale can exclude humans from pasts we reconstruct; the same is equally true for working at the micro-scale. Archaeological scientists have dominated research at the micro-scale with the use of microscopes, chemical analyses and other instruments. There is a tendency to ignore the humanness of the past and replace it instead with compositional analyses and microstructural characterisations. Scientists often get very excited about their results but it is important to remember that the results of such analyses are invariably small samples from a fragmentary assemblage that may be an insignificant element of the whole site. This is not to dismiss scientific analysis but more a cautionary note to remind us that work at the micro-scale is often difficult to realise at the human scale.

Such analyses have their role within archaeology but they should always be initiated from a good archaeological question. There is nothing more frustrating to archaeologists than to see scientists practising in the spirit of mountaineers; that is analysing things because they are there! If there is not a good reason for chopping a sample up, subjecting it to analysis, while absorbing much sought after funds, then it simply should not be done. If this

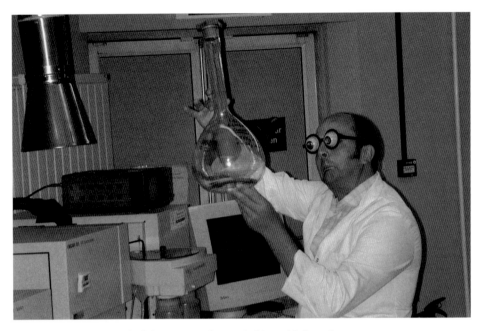

3 *The scientist in his cloak of objectivity worshipping in his empirical temple*

seems unbelievable then look at any excavation report or grand synthesis to see how much use of scientific analyses is actually made. You will most likely find such work relegated to the appendixes and even then hardly referred to. It is perhaps a little unfair to blame over-eager scientists sitting in labs dressed in their white cloaks of objectivity (**3**). The problem perhaps is caused by the organisation of the archaeological process that tends to send boxes of artefacts to scientists who are chained to their lab benches. Nonetheless, science-based approaches have been guilty of arrogance; they often claim that their investigations are more thorough and more objective. The rest of this chapter asks how exactly we might start to use science within archaeological practice in a more productive manner.

How can we analyse for power?

An ethereal concept such as power might seem beyond the means of investigation using scientific analysis. Power is made concrete through employment of artefacts, inhabitation of certain spaces and the acting out of certain practices. On a day-to-day basis we recognise different 'levels' of power often by how we perceive status and identity – although, of course, these can always be misleading. If we can construct patterns in terms of how spaces were occupied, the nature of the practices carried out within them and how artefacts were used, then we can begin to think about how these patterns relate to power and how values are constructed.

The most common scientific technique used to detect differences in the use of space is the chemical characterisation of soil. Other techniques include soil micromorphology, whereby microscopic residues in the soil not normally visible are observed under a microscope in the laboratory. One great thing about microscopic and chemical analyses is that the object of analysis – microscopic or chemical residues – is less vulnerable to taphonomic processes than macroscopic finds. Since large finds can be kicked about easily after their initial discard, their distribution may not be particularly specific to the practices that created them. This makes residues ideal units of analysis that can relate very precisely to certain practices.

Such data needs to be understood then interpreted in light of active inhabitation of the site. This highlights the problems with how archaeology is practised. Traditionally, an excavation is undertaken and then the finds are 'bagged up' and sent for analyses. As the site is 'written up' the results drift back from the lab to the report's appendices. The time scale for this can be anything from a year to decades. By this point the site has normally been destroyed either by the process of excavation or development meaning that the site cannot be revisited in light of the analytical data. We should ask why do scientists stay in their laboratories?

In general, scientists do not like getting their pristine white coats dirty; they feel more at home in their laboratories with their gleaming instruments and clean benches. It also satisfies management's idea of expert specialists; they should do a narrow range of tasks. Archaeologists, on the other hand, are never happier than when they are up to their armpits in mud working outdoors in the field (4). Archaeologists can thus experience inhabiting the spaces with which we are concerned whereas scientists never even get to see them. The nearest encounter they have with the past is often a zip-lock bag containing cleansed finds. Unless they can somehow get out of their laboratories into the field, the irrelevance of much scientific work is destined to be an enduring feature of archaeology.

Many of the techniques that scientists use involve huge pieces of equipment that need to be based in a laboratory. However, with increasing miniaturisation, many of these mammoth pieces of equipment are now portable and easily usable on site so that the archaeologist can be given feedback in minutes rather than years. This is not to suggest that technological innovation came to the rescue of archaeology. If it had, then we would expect to find scientists swarming around archaeological sites. The fact is that what really stimulated some scientists to go into the field were the theoretical shifts associated with the emphasis on studying human doings through spatial inhabitation.

Thus to analyse for power we have to look at the methodological relationship between scientific pursuits and the practice of archaeology. What is

4 *The archaeologist enjoying being mucky*

needed, as with any good archaeology, is a proper question with which to begin. Scientists, or better still, archaeologists versed in science, need to locate their practice on site and offer feedback to archaeologists as they dig; only then can we begin to understand how space is inhabited. Such ideals are high; it would require a major reorganisation of the archaeological process that would, at least to some degree, require government legislation. Nonetheless, research-driven projects have no excuse not to engage with such ideals. They are certainly worth striving for because, as we said earlier, if the investigation is not geared to understanding what the potential of being human was, then it probably is not worth pursuing in the first place!

Identity and specialisation

Perhaps the most productive way of examining the articulation of power in societies is to investigate the means by which identities are constructed. By identity we mean the way social factors converge around an individual or group to render them definable in terms of, amongst other things, status and practice.

Earlier we saw that craft specialisation is an important characteristic in Service's scheme of social categorisation. Craft production is one such practice that is central to the construction of identity. What exactly do we mean by craft specialisation? Craft specialisation simply refers to the way in which production or labour is organised within a polity. In segmentary societies craft production is mainly attended to at the household level in what is often called the *domestic mode of production.*

Characteristics of such organisation include variation in artefact form, production debris in dwelling areas and a high variability in raw material composition. It is not difficult to see how these characteristics arise. In societies, which are characterised as chiefdoms or states, it is typical to encounter some degree of centralisation in craft production. Some archaeologists see this as a general rule of thumb by which to measure social complexity. However, just because production is centralised, does not mean that a society is more complex or sophisticated. Often there are strategies by which production can be decentralised although still controlled from a powerful centre. However, societies fitting the label of state or chiefdom do so because they show evidence of centralised production, collective efforts for resource exploitation such as at mine and quarry sites, and a general intensification of production.

Specialisation need not be considered an all-or-nothing affair. It is quite possible that groups engage in agricultural production to some extent whilst, at other times, practicing craft production; such a scenario would still satisfy the criteria of a degree of craft specialisation. Equally, it might be that certain groups are disinherited from agricultural production and in turn spend their time dedicated to craft production. Specialisation can come about for a multitude of reasons and perhaps the issue to address is exactly how specialisation impacts on identity or how specialised craft workers are differentiated or differentiate themselves from others in that society.

Case study: forging identity in the Manx Iron Age

Introduction

Excavation at the Billown Quarry site, under the direction of Prof. Tim Darvill, was initiated by the discovery of Neolithic remains in the track of an advancing limestone quarry. The total excavation of the site has revealed finds from all periods with evidence from the Mesolithic through to the industrial period. A notable facet of the project is the manner in which scientific analysis has always been integrated during excavation. Since 1995 scientific specialists have either visited or been part of the project in order to excavate, take samples and to report back their findings frequently during the same period of excavation. The project makes facilities available to visiting scientists such as soil labs, microscope study areas and sample preparation facilities.

The preliminary results have been instrumental in informing excavation technique, and important lessons learnt regarding the integration of science and archaeology. It seems that taking scientists into the field may be the best way to ensure this. Being confronted by the imminence of the evidence of past activities has a splendid way of focusing the mind. Archaeologists and scientists find themselves standing in mud, trowels and test-tubes in hand, talking about the archaeology, the problems associated with digging it and what it can all mean. It is a pity that more archaeology is not organised like this, especially at a commercial level.

The Billown Quarry site

The Isle of Man is located in the middle of the Irish Sea (**5**). The island can be divided into three main topographic zones, a quaternary plain to the north yields to a mountainous interior comprised chiefly of slate. To the south, the mountains give way to a fertile rolling landscape which, in the region around Castletown, covers extensive carboniferous limestone pavements. The island is famous for its copper, lead and zinc mineralisation. The Billown Quarry site is located in the southern part of the island about 2.5km north of Castletown (**6**). It is located on a rolling hill in a rich archaeological landscape and seems to have occupied an enduring place in the minds of its inhabitants through time. The most prominent feature in this part of the island is the Iron Age hill fort, on the summit of South Barrule, which dominates any northerly view from the site (**7**). From Billown it is possible to see the precipitous cliffs of Bradda Head and much of the landscape as it tumbles down to the sea at Langness. Both these landmarks are a source of copper ore.

There are rich Neolithic remains at the site with evidence for various enclosing structures and the building of cult centres or shrines. Evidence for Bronze Age occupation in the form of a settlement comprises a large round

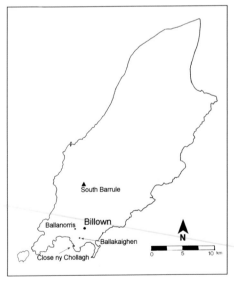

5   *Map showing the location of the Isle of Man*

6   *Map showing the location of the Billown Quarry site and other Iron Age sites*

7 *South Barrule, with its imposing summit, dominates the south of the island*

house with peripheral structures which may have been dwellings or associated with livestock. In time this settlement is eclipsed by a group of Iron Age 'dwellings' (**9**).

The Iron Age at Billown

In comparison with other periods at Billown, Iron Age occupation cannot be considered extensive. No ceramic evidence has been forthcoming for the Manx Iron Age and, across the island, the period is generally recognised as being aceramic.

Excavations in 1995 produced evidence of an enclosure with evidence of post holes and pits within it. Tim Darvill has identified this as a shrine structure. Excavations in 1999 investigated this feature with the opening of a new trench containing more Iron Age features. Iron Age remains can best be described as a nucleation of ring ditches, each approximately 7m in diameter. Dating by radiocarbon suggests the structures are contemporary with each other and of middle Iron Age date (414-384 BC). Two ring ditches have opposing entrances and seem to be associated suggesting that they were in someway related. It is clear that structure F630 is physically separated from these more nucleated structures. The first part of this case study relates to the investigations of this ring groove feature (F630). The finding of metallurgical debris including slag, crucibles, metal spillages and mould fragments during excavation within and around the structure suggests that it was in some way associated with metallurgy. One pressing question was where exactly was metal-working carried out? The scatter of slag and other debris suggested that it could have been either inside or outside of F630. It was also important to understand what kind of metallurgy was being practised at Billown: was it copper metallurgy, iron metallurgy or both? It was also important to think about the implications for those involved in these activities. For instance, could we comment on how these specific practices contributed to the construction of identity? Could we say whether their craft was specialised and how much of their time was spent doing it? By understanding the spatial articulation of metallurgy within F630 and how it related to its immediate and local community we might be able to gain insight into the social strategies employed by those working with metals and the influence this had on their power and identity.

Billown in its regional context

There is good evidence for Iron Age occupation in the immediate vicinity of Billown. Nearby are the rath-like structures of Ballacagen and Ballanorris (**8**). These large communal wood-built dwellings with turf roofs are thought to be contemporary with F630 at Billown. Such structures would have included an area for livestock as well as other activities. Both Ballacagen and Ballanorris have produced evidence for copper metallurgy in the form of casting dross and crucibles which are comparable with the crucible fragments excavated from F630.

Nearby to Ballacagen and Ballanorris is the promontory fort of Close Ny Chollagh. This is a spectacularly sited settlement situated on the coast over-looking Poyll Vaish. Several phases were identified at Close Ny Chollagh and, in the phase deemed to be contemporary with feature F630, evidence of crucibles and burnt mould or furnace fragments was found in one hut, suggesting copper metallurgy was being practised. Nearby is the hilltop of Chapel Hill, Balladoole which is enclosed by a substantial earthwork and an external ditch. The site has evidence of continuous occupation from the Mesolithic to the Christian period. No doubt occupation was sporadic but features include enclosures, cist graves, a Viking ship burial and a Christian *Keeill*. The Iron Age phase of this site is poorly understood and dating remains uncertain. No house plans were recovered from the enclosed area and finds were meagre with animal bones, shells, bone pins and fragments of metal from superficial contexts.

The only other certain Iron Age site worthy of mention is the hill fort of South Barrule which can also be considered roughly contemporary with the site of Billown, Ballanorris and Ballacagen and Close ny Chollagh. Carbon-14 dating suggests that the latest date of this site comes at the beginning of these other sites. South Barrule rises to a height of 484m and is the dominant landscape feature in the south of the island. The summit is marked by a prominent cairn and is enclosed by two concentric banks. Within this inner bank up to seventy hut circles have been identified and those excavated were found to comprise of stone and turf foundations defining an inner area approx-imately 6m in diameter. Three such houses, excavated by Peter Gelling in the

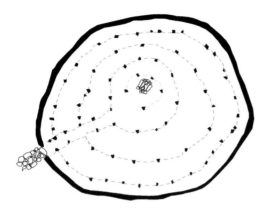

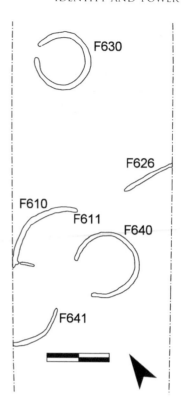

8   Above: *Plan of Ballacagen round house.* After Bersu, 1977

9   Right: *A plan showing the Iron Age remains at Billown.* Redrawn from Darvill, 1999

early 1960s, were found to have easterly oriented entrances, roughly paved floors and central hearths. All these sites are within about half a day's walk of one another and can be seen to represent a range of sites within the southern territory of the island.

Excavating Feature 630

The investigation of F630 attempted to understand the internal organisation of the feature by employing a fine-resolution magnetic susceptibility survey in conjunction with a detailed soil chemical survey (**10**). Both surveys covered the entire enclosed area and its immediate surroundings. Excavation proceeded by the setting up of a 10m grid and then sampling at 50cm intervals. A single floor layer was identified in F630 and was sampled routinely for environmental evidence using flotation. Finds were recorded in their precise find locations to facilitate subsequent distribution analysis.

The analytical work aimed to investigate the nature of the metal-working activities undertaken within F630 and develop an understanding of how space was partitioned and used within the structure. Such an approach is useful as it supplements understandings gleaned through excavation and artefact studies. Such an approach has the explicit intention of focusing on the spatial and contextual relationships among artefacts, residues and the structure.

10 *The excavation of Feature 630.* Photo: Tim Darvill

Scientific analysis: magnetic susceptibility survey
Magnetic susceptibility instruments are ideal for investigating areas suspected of being associated with metallurgy. Slag residues are extraordinarily susceptible to induced magnetic fields, making their presence easily detectable. Not only could magnetic susceptibility be used to determine the presence of magnetically susceptible material, it can also quantify the magnetic susceptibility. This means that the concentration of metal-working residues can be quantified in different samples. Of course, any prospective researcher needs to exercise caution here. You have to be sure that the material producing the response in the instrument is indeed a metal-working residue. It is only then that you can start to identify which samples have higher concentrations of residue and were therefore closely associated with the metal-working area. Iron-smithing produces a material called hammerscale (**11**). Hammerscale is either plate-like or spheroidal and is normally virtually pure magnetite (Fe_3O_4), which has a very high magnetic susceptibility. It is formed on the surface of hot iron when it is exposed to air, when the iron artefact is hit the hammerscale is forced off and falls to the floor. The great thing about hammerscale for archaeologists is that, unlike crucible fragments and large lumps of slag, which can be kicked around, hammerscale is small – rarely more than 3mm – and is produced in large quantities and tends to stay in the vicinity of where it was produced. It therefore acts as a good marker for iron-working activities. Although it is still a subject of investigation,

11 *Electron micrograph of hammerscale produced by ironworking.* Photo: David Starley

there is the suspicion that different types of hammerscale relate to different types of forging. Some investigators have indicated that, when an iron bloom (the spongy mass of iron and slag produced in primary smelting) is forged in order to consolidate the iron, the hammerscale formed is predominantly spheroidal whilst simple forging produces a platy hammerscale.

Throughout the course of magnetic susceptibility determination, numerous random samples were taken to ensure that high magnetic susceptibility readings did indeed correlate with high hammerscale concentrations. This is a simple check to undertake and simply involved dragging a magnet over a known weight of dried soil. If the recoverable hammerscale is higher in the samples with a higher magnetic susceptibility you know the assumption is safe.

It is usual to map data generated from magnetic susceptibility surveys using computers in order to review spatial variations. The subjective process of manipulating data at this stage can either enhance or obliterate any results; seemingly bland results can be manipulated to emphasise trivial features and that is without even resorting to other tricks. Although these manipulative processes are essential for effective presentation of data they are employed rather subjectively and are thus open to abuse. Often the raw data is not even published, so the reader only has the visual representation to judge the results by, which can be rather misleading. The lesson here is that such data can give brilliant insights but, be wary, do not necessarily take everything at face value!

The results from the magnetic susceptibility survey can be seen in **12**. It is quite clear that the magnetic susceptibility varies widely across the extent of F630. The highest magnetic susceptibilities are located in the western half of the feature and in the vicinity of the entrance, presumably representing discard. Another interesting feature of the results is the restrictive nature of the distribution. As mentioned above, hammerscale should tend to stay roughly where it is produced and the results here certainly suggest this is the case.

Soil chemistry

Soil samples contain very low levels of trace elements and need to be analysed by an instrument known as the Atomic Absorption Spectrometer (AAS) (**14**). This instrument relies on samples being introduced in a liquid form and it is thus essential to digest the sample first. The range of digestion options are varied and can be selected to optimise recovery from the geological or anthropogenic fraction of the soil. The technique employed in this study utilised a rapid soak extraction using EDTA. This allowed large sample numbers to be analysed in little time. The elements analysed were copper, zinc and lead.

As with the magnetic susceptibility data, appropriate software was used to present the data. The results for zinc and lead showed little discernable variation and were deemed of little interpretative value, while the results from copper were dramatic and complimented the magnetic susceptibility results. The results for copper analyses can be seen in **13**. These two sets of results seemed to suggest that metallurgical activity was concentrated in the western flank of F630 with discarded residues in the entrance.

There is one important point about soil studies. Determining that the soil sample contains 120ppm copper does not really tell you anything. This is as true for a single sample as it is for a suite of samples. In the case illustrated here it was quite apparent from the type of finds recovered that metalworking was

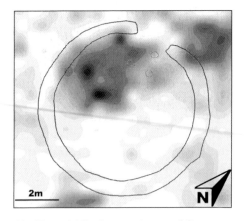

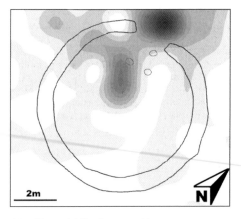

12 *The variability in magnetic susceptibility across F630*

13 *The variability in extractable copper concentration across F630*

Atomic Absorption Spectrometry

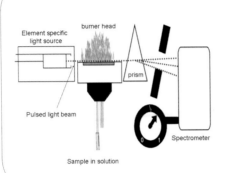

Element specific light source
burner head
prism
Pulsed light beam
Spectrometer
Sample in solution

Technique

Atomic Absorption Spectrometry has largely been eclipsed by ICP-AES but is still useful in archaeology. AAS is used for trace element analysis (TEA) for many materials including ceramics, lithics, metals and soils. The sample is introduced in to an acetylene flame at 3000°C, through which is shone a beam of light from a element specific lamp. Atoms excited by the flame and of the type being analysed will then absorb some of the light. By measuring the amount of light absorbed the concentration can be inferred.

Sampling

Most samples can be analysed by drilling 100mg of material. This should be considered a minimum sample size but larger samples are desirable. All AAS's require samples in the form of a fluid.

Dissolving samples can be difficult and time consuming because of method development. It is for this reason that AAS is better employed in routine analyses with high sample volumes.

Silicate materials are particularly difficult requiring complex digestion methods involving hydrofluoric acid or high temperature fusing with appropriate fluxes. Once dissolved the sample should be analysed rapidly as precipitation of solutions deteriorates precision and instrument function. Unlike microscopic techniques where the sample can be archived, solutions for analysis by AAS are destroyed in the process of analysis.

Applications

AAS offers an easily available and economic means of TEA. It is a robust and well-developed technique. These advantages are offset by the time taken for analysis. It is usual that only a single element can be determined at a time making for lengthy analysis campaigns. AAS is limited to the analysis of metal atoms whilst its precision is often an order of magnitude worse than ICP. It is used in provenance and for materials characterisation as well as basic soil chemistry studies.

A typical AAS instrument being used for provenance studies

being practised somewhere in the vicinity of the feature. In the absence of these finds, that is slag, crucibles, moulds and metal spillages, soil-analysis results would have been difficult to interpret. It is true that internal divisions could have been identified but not attributed with a function. We are heavily reliant on archaeological evidence and hence archaeological interpretation in the formulation of our 'supposedly' objective scientific research programme. In some ways F630 is an exceptional example to use to illustrate the worth of soil chemical studies. In this case we have a very firm impression of what sort of activities were being practised because of the artefact assemblage found in and around the structure. It should of course be remembered that metalworking may only represent one of the activities taking place in F630. In light of this we should perhaps not see soil chemical analyses as being an alternative to conventional artefact analyses, rather they are complimentary approaches which, when combined, can assist us in understanding how space was utilised and even how this differed through time.

Production debris analysis
As mentioned earlier, excavation of F630 produced a large assemblage of metal-working debris including slag, crucible fragments, moulds and metal spillages. Visual examination allowed these finds to be divided into two main groups: debris relating to the melting and casting of copper alloy on one hand and debris relating to the smithing of iron on the other. The proximity of these finds suggests that the same people worked iron and copper, which calls into question our ideas of specialisation based on terms like blacksmithing and coppersmithing.

Metallurgical finds were analysed using reflected light microscopy (**15**) and Scanning Electron Microscopy (SEM) in conjunction with an EDS facility (**16**). The main conclusions from metallographic and microprobe analysis of the metallurgical production debris are that, although ironworking and copperworking took place in close proximity, they did not take place simulta-neously. This is deduced from the fact that there was no evidence of copper inclusions in the ironsmithing slag. Reasons for this separation may rest in the domain of the practical but it is equally plausible that they extend to include ideas relating to social or ideological issues.

Analysis of crucible fragments identified a consistent alloy composition was being used which was unusual compared to the mainland (**17**), containing no tin or lead and with a trace of arsenic. Some prills of silver were also noted which suggests copper was not the only metal cast at Billown.

Craft specialisation and identity in the Manx Iron Age
Within Iron Age studies much attention has been paid to how the organisation of domestic space both creates and reflects cosmological concerns. Recently, much attention has focused on the orientation of Iron Age house entrances and it is suggested that the daily transit of the sun illuminates areas of the 'house'

Reflected light microscopy

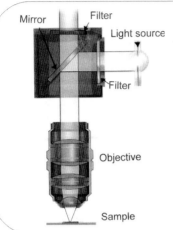

Mirror
Filter
Light source
Filter
Objective
Sample

Technique

RLM illuminates opaque solid surfaces by directing light through the microscope objective and reflecting it back to the eyepiece. The minimum feature resolution is 0.2 microns. Polarised light, interference contrast and dark field illumination methods can all help to resolve aspects of sample detail and microstructure. Bright field mode produces true colour images at magnifications of up to 1500x. Reflective surfaces perpendicular appear bright, non-reflective features or oblique features reflect less light and appear darker. Polarising lenses can be introduced to the optical path to study features with anisotropic refractive properties. Dark field illumination enhances contrasts for subtle topographic features.

Sampling

Samples of objects of interest are cut and polished to enable detailed examination of microstructural detail. Small samples can be prepared, whilst larger samples are removed from larger objects and cut to size with a diamond saw. The sample is impregnated with resin and placed in a block with the surface of interest oriented towards the polishing surface.

The sample is then ground and polished with successively finer grades of alumina and diamond pastes to achieve a flat clean surface.

The same sample above is seen in bright field illumination on the left and darkfield on the right. This pottery is coated with a slip layer that appears as one uniform layer in bright field, but subtleties of texture are revealed in darkfield as two separate slip layers.

Applications

Reflected light microscopy can be used to study the microstructural detail of almost all sample types. It is particularly useful for examining polished cross sections of solid materials such as metals, lithics and ceramics as well as debris from technological processes. Samples prepared for RLM can also be examined and analysed using SEM-EDS. RLM is used for preliminary examination of samples for the selection of areas to analyse with other techniques such as SEM work.

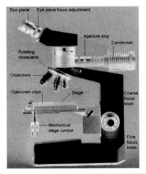

SEM-EDS

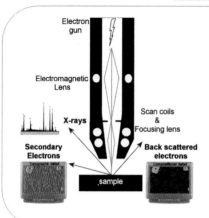

Technique

Scanning electron microscopy, when used in conjunction with X-ray analysis (SEM-EDS) is among the most useful techniques available to the archaeologist. An electron beam illuminates the sample and induces secondary (SE) and backscattered (BSE) electrons and X-rays. SE provide high quality topographic images whilst BSE allows images based on differences in atomic density. Chemical analysis is undertaken by measuring the energy and intensity of the X-rays formed. It is possible manipulate the beam to analyse very small samples.

Sampling

Samples larger than 1cm^3 need little preparation apart from cleaning. Smaller samples are mounted in a resin or on mounting compound. Samples can either be prepared (see Figs 2.1 and 2.14) or 'rough', with original surface in tact. Modern SEM-EDS instruments have large chambers allowing whole artefacts to be investigated without sampling. However if chemical analysis is required a fresh section is normally made. Imaging is degraded by static build-up so samples must be coated in either gold or carbon. Carbon would normally be used if analyses were required in addition to images.

Examining a polished section by SEM-EDS

Applications

Wide-ranging application, useful for the imaging and analysis of a variety of materials. X-ray analysis can detect elements heavier than carbon when they are present in excess of ~0.5wt%. They are rarely used for provenance studies being much better suited to issues of technological choice and materials characterisation.

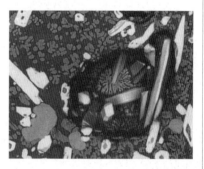

Bell founding waste. This high contrast image was taken using BSE. The heavy mineral species are white (tin oxide) whilst the silica rich phases are dark. Note the excellent depth of field possible with a SEM-EDS

sequentially; this, in turn, creates a scheme by which different practices are attributed to different spaces. Andrew Fitzpatrick suggests that the orientations of wheel-house entrances are explicitly associated with cosmological concerns and he describes a mechanism linking use of space with sleep and death (right-handed) and life with food preparation and production (left-handed) (18).

With this in mind the findings from F630 can be considered as being far from 'normal'. The entrance of the structure is elaborate and faces north–north–west neatly framing the summit of South Barrule. A survey of Manx, Cumbrian, Lancashire, and North Welsh sites found that over 80 per cent of entrances face east to southeast, their position to sunrise presumably being critical. It seems reasonable that there would be a degree of familiarity for most individuals entering most Iron Age 'houses'. In comparison, entering F630 would be peculiar. Not only is the entrance orientated to ensure that at no time in the day does the sun shine directly into it, but, additionally, the practices within the structure are not typical. Anyone anticipating the organisation of space within such a structure would, upon entry, be quite disorientated by the skewed hand-edness of the inside, production being in this case on the right-hand side of the individual entering. During excavation the highest concentration of slag debris was found around the threshold of the structure that would have perhaps advertised the activities going on within to those outside.

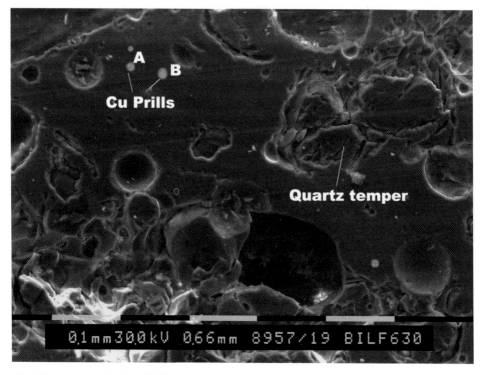

17 *Electronmicrograph of crucible fragment*

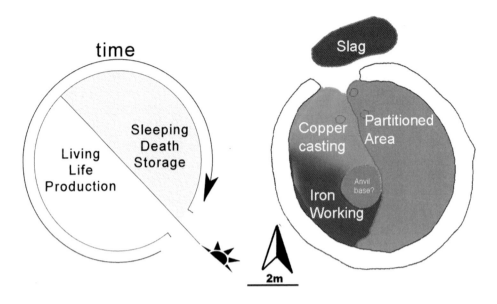

18 *Ideas of symbolic space in Iron Age dwellings*

It has been suggested that roundhouses associated with metallurgy, had elaborate entrances to ensure dim light for working hot glowing metal. Nevertheless, even if entrance orientation was determined by functional concerns to better facilitate metallurgy, it is probable that other symbolic connotations would soon have been woven into people's understandings of this structure and its inhabitants. The peculiar orientation, the unusual slag accumulations, the sounds and sparks emanating from this structure would all have impacted on people's impression of place and its inhabitants. In turn these impressions would have been powerful forces in constructing the identities of those who occupied it.

Evidence for copper-alloy-working was found at numerous sites near to Billown including Close ny Chollagh, Ballacagen and Ballanorris. That these sites are contemporary, communal and domestic suggests that copperworking cannot be considered an unusual activity. For copper metallurgy, it seems, at this point in Manx history each community tended to its own needs.

Iron metallurgy, on the other hand, seems to be much more restricted. Only Billown provides evidence for iron metallurgy suggesting control over its distribution. The restricted peripheral space at Billown strongly contrasts with the open areas at Ballacagen and Ballanorris. Such observations allow us to consider the relative value of materials. Contrasting the case for copper and iron pins, an artefact used for display in dress illustrates this point. Copper pins were most likely made at sites where they were consumed. Its public production means that its moment of 'birth' would have been witnessed and perhaps also the 'death' of any artefacts melted down to create it. The style and material used for such pins would probably indicate small group identities at the level of the site. Iron pins, which would have served similar uses in dress display, would have had a very different biography. Not created in a public place nor the product of a commonly witnessed skill, these would have appeared unusual, differences possibly signifying ideas beyond the immediate group and making reference to the strange behaviours at Billown, itself a place that seems to have occupied an enduring image in the minds of people since the Mesolithic. Through considering the regional evidence, relative material values can be considered and a mechanism appreciated for how the actions of the smiths at Billown extend beyond the physicality of their own bodies.

Conclusions

The concept of the magical, outcast or marginalised smith, somehow on the edge of society or, at least, someone with special powers to be treated differently, is a common one. The study presented here shows that it is only when we start to understand how the organisation of space and architecture are linked with dramatic practices and how individual perceptions of these are woven together, that we start to understand how individuals such as smiths may have begun to acquire their special identitys which have proven to be so enduring.

Reviewing the history of technological studies within archaeology, as practised in the West, reveals a polarised discourse with ideas relating to either technological determinism on one hand, or technological somnambulism on the other. The difficulty archaeologists have had in being able to relate scientific studies of technology to social aspects of the past is a direct result of adhering to a overly scientist idea of technology. The work undertaken on F630 was part of a wider agenda for the Billown Landscape Project to revise our understandings and methodologies of how to study the remains of ancient production.

Central to the study of metallurgical debris has always been the attempt to characterise the nature of the processes responsible for their formation. To this end, the study of production debris here differs little from traditional approaches. However, when such studies are combined with soil studies and undertaken within a research agenda that questions issues beyond mere technological characterisation and description, useful inferences can be made about issues such as specialisation and identity. Metallurgy has traditionally been studied within an intellectual paradigm that emphasises the evolution of metallurgical processes, the efficiency of the techniques employed and the mechanical advantages offered by the products. In adopting such an approach the role of the individual craftsperson is de-emphasised with the effect that technological studies are often deemed of only marginal interest to wider archaeological practice.

3

ORGANISING PRODUCTION

Death and production

Archaeologists interested in working out how a society was organised often look at burials as indicators of status, identity and expressions of power. Death, however, distorts social realities. The treatment of the dead in funerary practice is susceptible to the cultural distortion of the living. Nonetheless, when archaeologists think about and investigate past social organisation, they tend to flock to cemeteries. We would argue that the arenas of the living are just as valid units of study. How we make objects is one of the keys to understanding the sort of society we live in. Production processes of a whole range of everyday items are caught up within processes of resource access, political, economic and cultural factors that help to determine the character of innovation, production and consumption. Studying technologies and how they were organised can therefore give important insights about how social life itself was organised.

The mode of production

The mode of production models independently developed by David Peacock and Van der Leeuw differentiate between household or domestic production and several modes of specialised production: household industry; individual workshop industry; nucleated workshop industry; the manufactory. Each mode is defined by a particular configuration of variable factors. These include: the frequency, intensity and seasonality of production; the number and sex of the workers together with their age and status relationships; the extent of labour division; the degree of investment in specialist equipment such as kilns or furnaces; the variability in the raw materials exploited and in the range of artefacts produced. Each mode is summarised by **19**.

In reality the mode of production is infinitely variable, with many examples falling between, rather than within, these modes. Some view the model of mode of production as evolutionary and thus implicitly formalistic. Chris Cumberpatch has proposed a redefinition of the term 'mode of production' which, whilst retaining the fundamental pivot between forces and relations of production, operates at a methodological level rather than as formalistic social theory.

The mode of production redefined

A scheme developed by Chris Cumberpatch defines the elements, or 'components', of any mode of production as:

- Raw material
- Labour
- Technology
- Output

Components and variables	HOUSEHOLD PRODUCTION	HOUSEHOLD INDUSTRY	INDIVIDUAL WORKSHOP	NUCLEATED WORKSHOP	MANUFACTORY
RAW MATERIAL					
Procurement	Haphazard	Increasingly regular	Regular use of known sources with increase in processing	Regular use of known sources with advanced processing such as levigation elutriation, grinding, etc.	Use of known sources with well known properties
Processing	Minimum	Minimum			
LABOUR					
Division/ Organisation	Individual	Individual	Family group	Highly organised	Production processes are specialised so that there are many workers in a labour
Intensity (specialisation)	Low	Low specialisation	Individual specialist knowledge	High degree of specialism Several full-time workers with internal hierarchy	force with specialist division of labour. Peacock gives an arbitrary figure of 12 or more
Number of workers	Few	Few	Rising		
Seasonality	High	High	Low	Low seasonality	Non-seasonal
TECHNOLOGY					
Complexity/ investment	Low/Low	Low-rising (e.g. turntable)	Permanent facilities workshop, wheel, kiln levigation tanks or similar preparation facilities and	High investment in permanent facilities such as workshops, drying sheds, kilns etc.	High investment in permanent facilities
Techniques of production	Simple	Low-rising	increasing number of production steps involved	Complex sequence of production with possible division of labour	Production steps tailored to maximum output
OUTPUT					
Quantity	Low	Low-rising	Rising	High	High
Variability	High	High	Low- standard range	Specific range of products	Very low variability

19 *Mode of production table*

These components are essential to all modes of production, being fundamental to the process in the sense that, in the absence of any, production could not take place. Each component can also be considered with reference to variables such as the division and intensity of labour involved or the procurement and processing necessary in obtaining raw materials. The components and variables comprising a mode of production are seen in **20**.

In this scheme, society is not dominated or defined by a single mode of production, rather a given social formation can be seen as being composed of a coincidence of modes of production which will vary owing to particular historical circumstances. It can be envisaged that a number of modes of production will increase during periods of transition or in societies that are especially complex or interactive with others. Thus an additional complexity of the articulation among different modes of production can be seen whilst the social component of each remains integral.

In practice the investigation of such articulating modes of production requires the detailed examination of the entire assemblages of different artefact types from metals, stone and bone, to glass, tile and brick from a series of sites within a given region. The methodology used to define a mode of artefact production has to be based on detailed examination of the artefacts involved from the point of view of production technology. The aim is to reconstruct, as fully as possible, the components and variables which were involved in the manufacture of the artefacts. We can suggest a mode of production for any given artefact based on a detailed knowledge of what and how it was made. Once the technological characteristics of an artefact have been defined by detailed analyses, the sequences of its production can be described. The remaining variables consti-

Components	Variables
Raw materials	Procurement (including transport) Processing
Labour	Division/organisation Intensity Number of labourers involved Seasonality
Technology	Complexity/investment Sequence/techniques of production
Output	Quantity Variability

20 *Components and variables of the mode of production.* After Cumberpatch, 1991

tuting the mode of production can then be considered from an ethnographic and inferential viewpoint, (with reference for example to the ethnographically based models described in **19**) which will serve to suggest definition of those variables which are largely invisible in the archaeological record.

Case study: the enigma of the Eastern Alpine metallurgical process

Introduction

For nearly five millennia, individuals have exploited the band of copper mineralisation that runs east-west through the middle of the Austrian Alps (**21**). In the Mitterberg region as early as the nineteenth century archaeologists had started to record evidence of 'old men workings'. This long tradition of academic enquiry probably makes the remains of prehistoric copper mining and smelting in the Eastern Alps the most heavily studied prehistoric metallurgical remains in the world. Despite copious archaeological and scientific work, no coherent understanding of copper production has emerged from the mound of published literature. Contradictory accounts deal with the same site or assemblage. This state of confusion has made some leading scholars declare that this area requires yet more study, whilst others have simply chosen to ignore this important strand of European prehistory in general archaeological narratives.

Considering the amount of research already conducted in this area it seems unlikely that resorting to test tubes or trowels will solve anything. We have

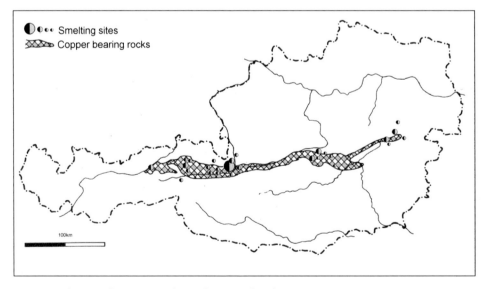

21　*Map of Austria showing zone of mineralisation and smelting sites*

already discussed the idea that the past does not emerge from the mists of time with ever-increasing description, be it archaeological or scientific. Rather, future insights will come through better understanding the nature of the questions that we ask. Nowhere is this point more relevant than in the study of the 'Eastern Alpine metallurgical process'. The key question archaeologists and scientists have asked of this body of evidence is 'What is the nature of the Eastern Alpine metallurgical process?'

Choosing to investigate 'The Eastern Alpine metallurgical process' is itself revealing, the name implies that there existed a single process capable of accounting for the archaeological remains that stretch over several thousand square kilometres and over nearly two millennia. It is this problem that is dealt with in this case study.

History of analytical frameworks

The intensity of excavation in the Eastern Alps at copper smelting and mining sites has been matched by an equal intensity of archaeometric research. Such studies have documented the form of mining sites, furnaces and roasting beds, and the chemistry and microstructure of slag. The goal of these investigations has been to date the site and to identify the technical and chemical pathways by which the raw material was converted into copper. Excavations undertaken across the Alpine region have shown that many features encountered share structural similarities. Roasting beds, structures presumably used to pre-treat minerals, have been found to be consistently 0.9m in width, though varying in length from 2 to over 15m. Their construction seems remarkably similar

22 *An example of an Eastern-Alpine smelting furnace*

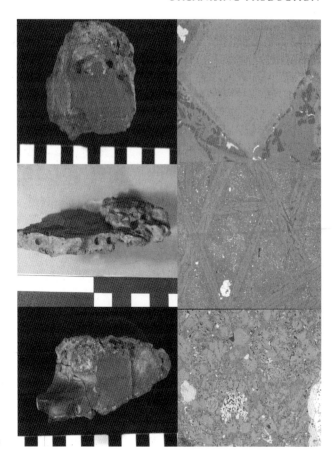

23 *Common Alpine slag types with corresponding microstructures*

comprising a deeply burnt area bounded by vertically placed stones. Likewise, furnaces appear to share many similarities (**22**). They invariably have a sub-rectangular cross-section, varying in diameter from 1.2m to 0.4m and survive in height from 0.5m to 0.9m. Usually, they are built into a low terrace or slope and are constructed of schist blocks cemented together with clay. It is usual to find the internal surfaces vitrified and covered in slag up to 2cm thick. In front of many furnaces large schist blocks covered in burnt clay have been found that could have been a front wall. Excavation normally finds these as a collapsed scatter of burnt stone and clay. The similarities in furnace form and construction are mirrored in the morphology of the slag. Three main slag morphologies are found on most sites: a thin plate slag, a thick dense slag and a vesicular slag (**23**). On some sites a fourth kind of slag deposit is found, sand slag, which seems to be the product of grinding, probably to recover copper prills or to use in other applications such as a pot temper.

This similarity in slag and furnaces from different sites has suggested to some scholars that these sites employ common techniques and thus represent evidence for an Eastern Alpine metallurgical process. Such observations stimulated the

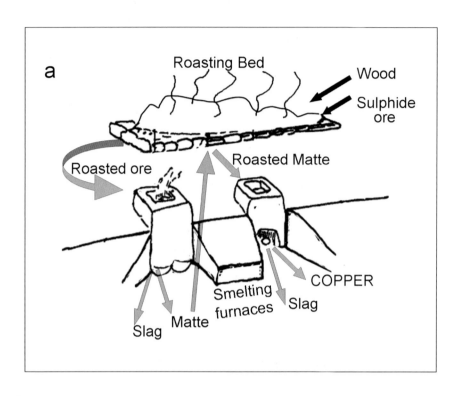

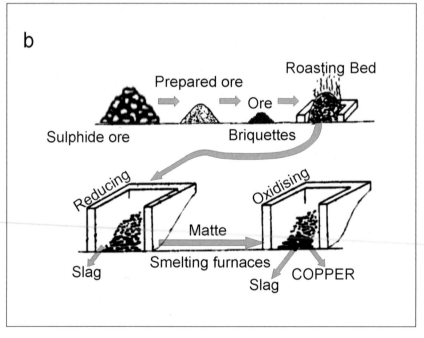

24 *Two models to account for the Eastern-Alpine metallurgical process.* Based on Presslinger and Eibner, 1988 and Moesta, 1986

search for the enigmatic 'Eastern Alpine metallurgical process' that has coloured archaeometric research in this area ever since. The similarity encountered in the structure of furnaces, their spatial articulation and slag morphology has not been matched in the results of archaeometric enquiry. The confusion that surrounds this whole area of study is rooted in archaeometric analyses. Scientists trying to define the technical and chemical pathway for the process have found themselves immersed in contention. Starting at the site level they have defined a pathway for the evidence to hand but, when comparing it to models derived from other sites, have found themselves in disagreement. Herein lies the confusion in this particular area of study. The variation in proposed models is stark ranging from processes which are oxidising conducted in furnaces without front walls to others which are reducing and carried out in tall shaft furnaces with front walls (24). Numerous attempts have been made to resolve these differences including more excavation, further analyses and even full-scale experimental reconstruction (25). However, it seems that the variation in analytical results refuse to be shoe-horned into a single model that can be called the 'Eastern Alpine metallurgical process'.

The assumption that a single process can account for all metallurgical remains over such large spans of time and space holds within it the implicit suggestion that the Alpine region was occupied by a coherent ethnic group or was even under the control of some sort of autonomous state.

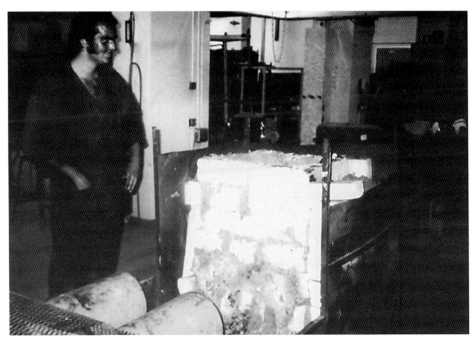

25 *Reconstructing the technical aspects of the 'Eastern-Alpine metallurgical process'*

A reassessment of the copper smelting in the Alpine Bronze Age

Alpine copper smelting invariably exploited primary sulphide ores, namely chalcopyrite or fahlerz ores. From a technical or chemical standpoint, the choices involved in transforming secondary oxide ores into metal are relatively limited when compared to the transformation of sulphide ores. This greater opportunity for choice and possible solutions means that one may expect technological systems for sulphide smelting to appear more diverse from different cultures than perhaps is the case for oxide-ore smelting. At the risk of over simplifying these alternative strategies, the key difference between them is whether or not the smelting stage takes place in a reducing or oxidising atmosphere. Contradictions in models relating to 'The Eastern Alpine Metallurgical Process' concern furnace chemistry. In fact, most models really only address furnace chemistry and the reactions of the smelted minerals.

Against a research culture obsessed with defining chemical pathways, stands the work of Prof. Clemens Eibner. Although he has also proposed a technical model for the production of copper, he has created a furnace typology and seriated numerous examples (26). The true importance of this typology is that it is one of the few examples of scholastic work that suggests that Alpine copper-smelting technology changed through time. Unfortunately, the implication of these changes has not been developed. It is argued here that these changes are central to understanding Alpine copper smelting in the Bronze Age.

Eibner's furnace typology shows that furnace dimensions decrease through time. However, the basic morphological unit and the general technique of construction appear to be maintained. Paralleling changes in furnace size, roasting beds decrease in size from 18m to 2m in length. Despite these huge changes in 'architectural' proportions, the significance has never been discussed in terms of what this means for practice.

The concept of furnace architecture is an important one. Too often technological remains are referred to as merely 'features' rather than architecture. The use of the term 'feature' to describe architecture with a technological function effectively relegates it to a position of lesser importance than other architecture. This is symptomatic of the prejudice against technological studies within archaeology and reinforces the erroneous set of beliefs that render technology somehow outside of society and hence of little interest to archaeology. Acknowledging technological structures as architecture allows us to think in terms of the way people moved around them, interacted with them and how they employed them as a resource in recreating the act of copper smelting; it opens them up for architectural and spatial analysis.

Admittedly, furnaces are a peculiar form of architecture, people cannot move through them in the normal sense but, nevertheless, they enclose an environment which humans control and manipulate, drawing on their knowledge, expectations and memories of smelting, to transform brittle

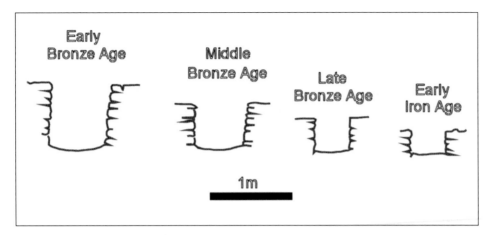

26 *Eibner's furnace typology showing change through time*

stones to malleable shiny metal. When engaged in excavation of these furnaces or in experimental reconstructions, we have the opportunity to inhabit the same kind of space as people did in the past. This gives us the chance to explore possible encounters with the furnace in relation to our bodies and such analysis brings us a step nearer to looking at metallurgy on a scale directly relevant to human experience.

Approaching an Alpine furnace one is confronted with a working space that is different at distinct periods in time. Early furnaces can be up to 1.2m wide whilst later furnaces may be as little as 0.4m. These different sizes have implications for the possible ways space is inhabited and the architecture encountered.

Movement is relatively free around earlier, larger furnaces: there is ample room for three or possibly four adults on the anterior working platform (**27**). It is from this position that the environment within the furnace would have been controlled through the use of bellows. When situated in this space, it is obvious that the furnace is out of reach of one pair of hands. It is, therefore, impossible to envisage how one can engage with such a furnace without the assistance of several others. Evidence for the use of multiple bellows comes from the excavation of *in situ* tuyere fragments. This experience is in direct contrast with the experience of approaching a later Bronze Age or Urnfield period furnace. In this case one becomes aware of the lack of choice in terms of where to place oneself, as though the furnace itself reaches out, forcing you to engage with it: it is obvious that it would not be possible to have more than two people in this space.

Choosing to interpret these architectural changes in terms of the number of adult people who could have worked at the front of the furnace, forces us to think in terms of action, group size and the organisation of labour. It could be that changes in architectural dimension reflect something else, bellow

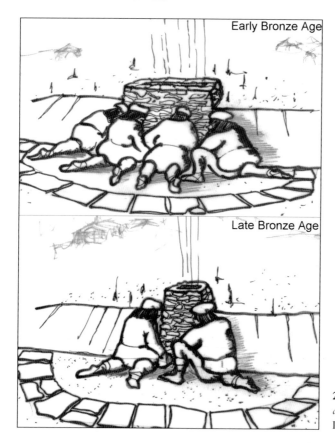

Early Bronze Age

Late Bronze Age

27 *The inhabitation of space around different furnace forms.* Drawing: M.Barnes

design for instance. Of course this remains possible but changes in furnace dimensions and the implication for smelting group size is also reflected in the structures termed roasting beds (see above). Furthermore, bellow design must be seen as being more conservative than furnace design for simple reasons. Firstly, whereas a furnace may have been rebuilt after each smelt, bellows may have lasted for several generations, if cared for correctly. This means that the opportunity for innovation or change in form is many times higher for furnaces than for bellows.

Based on analysis of architectural evidence, Alpine copper smelting changes through time, from a scenario where many individuals worked at the furnace to one later where no more than two worked at the furnace anterior. If the change in roasting bed size is also considered in terms of embodied experience, then there is ample evidence to support the idea of a change from a large group to smaller group activity.

Such a change is not inconsistent with other changes seen to occur in the European Bronze Age. The Bronze Age is often characterised by increasing specialisation, although such general statements ignore specific local events. Broad changes have been characterised as a movement from a society which emphasised the past and the community to one which emphasised individuals in the form of separate burials, the accumulation of a surplus and hence a preoccupation with the present and craft production. Invariably these changes are inferred by evidence from burials, the common ground for archaeologists, since artefacts from these contexts lend themselves to traditional archaeological categorisation. The change in Alpine metallurgical architecture is direct evidence that the social organisation of labour changed, suggesting that metal production became increasingly specialised, changing from a large group to a smaller more intensive group activity. It is important to emphasise that this change in smelting group size is not a response to changes in geological phenomena but rather the outcome of complex social changes involving the organisation of labour in the second millennium BC.

These architectural changes are not the only ones associated with copper smelting. Accompanying the change to a smaller group activity is a change in the distribution and number of smelting sites. Preliminary impressions are that the number of later sites dramatically outnumber earlier sites. In later periods, sites are considerably smaller as production appears more concentrated, although the distribution of these sites increases. Changes in site distribution and frequency suggest the location of production changes from a single, large, central site to multiple sites dispersed along Alpine valleys. This is an apparent decentralisation that is at odds with our understanding of changes elsewhere in Bronze Age society. Centralisation of storage and production is an obvious strategy that offers advantages for resource control and access. The apparent decentralisation of Alpine copper production must therefore be considered odd, especially as it is the control of metals which so often has been argued as central to élite dominance. Since so many copper artefacts are found in contexts suggesting their deposition was part of a social practice responsible for reinforcing the role of élite groups, we must assume that somehow control was exercised over this resource. The question then arises; if it was not through the centralisation of production, how was the production of metals controlled in the later Alpine Bronze Age?

Central to understanding changes in the organisation of production are the variations in process chemistry that so confused archaeometric studies in search of a single Alpine metallurgical process. Changes in furnace architecture correlate with changes in furnace chemistry. It seems an unintended consequence of reorganising labour was a change in furnace architecture that, in turn, changed the process chemistry. Changes in furnace design to accommodate the smaller smelting group size affected the chemistry of smelting which was, in turn, taken advantage of by the empowered élite as a means by which they could control production.

In all the confusion of competing chemical models to account for the enigmatic Alpine metallurgical process, nobody noted that models that were based on data from early sites were oxidising processes and undertaken in a single step. This contrasted with models derived from later sites where the process seemed to be reducing and involved multiple distinct steps to produce copper. For later sites, chemical and microstructural analysis has shown that the most common kind of metallic inclusion in slag is matte (**28**), a copper iron sulphide, which can be considered as an intermediate product between ore and finished copper. Evidence appears to be lacking for exactly how copper was produced at these later sites as matte seems to be the most common product. Matte can be considered inherently valuable as it has a high copper content, although effectively useless until it has undergone a final stage of conversion under oxidising conditions to form copper metal.

It seems that there never was a single Eastern Alpine metallurgical process. Rather the unintended consequences of the reorganisation of labour in the Middle Bronze Age was responsible for the decrease in furnace size with the effect that the smelting process changed from a single-step oxidising process to a reducing multi-step process which produced a useless yet valuable intermediate. The transition from a single to multiple step process facilitated alternative strategies for resource control. There is some evidence to suggest in the later Bronze Age that the final conversion of matte to copper was centralised and under the control of an élite who conducted the act maybe in secret or associated it with taboos so that they were not challenged by others carrying out illicit conversions elsewhere. It seems that the apparent decentralisation of primary production was therefore possible without any loss of resource control as access to copper was only possible with the knowledge and resources necessary to bring about the final stage of conversion.

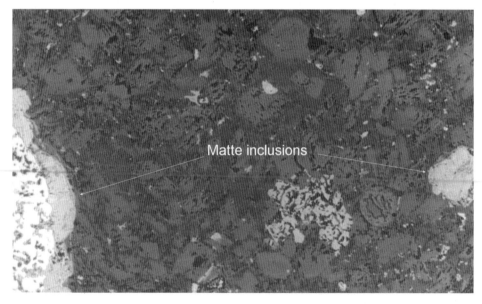

28 *Photomicrograph showing presence of matte inclusions in slag*

Escaping from the Alpine metallurgical process

This case clearly demonstrates how decisions made in non-technical spheres of society can have effects on technical factors such as smelting chemistry. This emphasises the sociological basis of technology and shows that technological studies must be viewed as valid subjects of anthropological study. Such understandings of technology are possible when technological features are subjected to architectural analysis, such practices are critical if chemical data is to be reworked or explained at the human scale. The discussion presented here has attempted to demonstrate the fully social nature of technology and, simultaneously, arbitrate between apparently conflicting evidence to offer a more meaningful explanation of the technological remains found in the Alpine Bronze Age.

Case study: slip-decorated pottery in Iron Age France

Introduction

In the previous case study the importance of production context was emphasised, including the value of exploring the spaces and technological architectures that craftspeople inhabit as they perform the gestures that animate production. The present case study provides a contrast in that the more usual archaeological situation of a lack of evidence of production sites prevails. How can archaeologists use archaeological science to help understand the organisation of ancient production processes and issues of craft specialisation when all we have are the fragmentary remains of the products of those processes?

The Auvergne Archaeological Survey (**29**), directed by John Collis, aimed to challenge the accepted focus of excavations of nucleated settlements known as *oppida* that had dominated the archaeology of the Iron Age. Interest was turned to investigate what was happening in the hinterlands of these famous 'urban' centres. Survey revealed a landscape teaming with evidence for agricultural, ritual and industrial activities where previous generations of archaeologists had not looked, distracted as they were by the massive nucleated *oppida*. The site of Aulnat has been described as an 'industrial village' with evidence for the manufacture of almost all artefact types from bone-combs, leather-work and metal-work, to glass beads – but, intriguingly, very little evidence for the manufacture of pottery. The site has yielded, however, one of the largest collections in the area of fineware pottery of various types but principally slip-decorated or 'painted' pottery. Archaeometric analysis of the pottery has allowed a detailed understanding of the sequences and modes of pottery production. It has also revealed the sophisticated decorative repertoires of the potters. Stunningly beautiful artistry seems to have been performed using sophisticated techniques that challenge even our own concepts of specialisation. Detailed analysis of the production processes have also suggested that

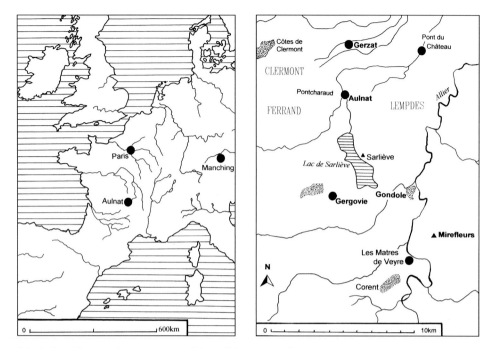

29 Left: *Aulnat in relation to Paris and the well-known site of Manching in Bavaria.* Right: *The sites of Aulnat and Gerzat in relation to the Auvergne area, in particular the* oppidum *site of Gergovie (the 'capital' of the Auvergni tribe) and Les Matres de Veyre, which became a major pottery production centre following the Roman conquest of Gaul*

markedly different pottery types with contrasting decoration were probably closely related in terms of the methods and rhythms of their production.

Slip-decorated pottery

Vessel sherds of the slip-decorated pottery class are characterised by their decorative surfaces which are composed of various combinations of differently coloured slips. The fragmentary condition of the Aulnat assemblage has limited those observations which could be made concerning the size and shape of the slip-decorated vessels. Examination of the fragmentary rim, body and bases from the assemblage indicates two main vessel forms: out-turn rimmed, closed vases (**30**) and in-turn rimmed open bowls, with no evidence for any handles or perforations. Slip-decorated pottery was made on a fast wheel of a fine, micaceous body fabric containing inclusions, most commonly quartz. The most common colours of slip decorations are reds and whites and more rarely mauve/greys, which appear as black on better preserved, for example water-logged specimens. Three main colour groups were identified: bright 'paper' white an 'off white', cream colour; orange/red. A fourth colour, the mauve/grey was often very thin and ephemeral. This colour was used to paint on bold designs, not all of which have survived (**31**).

A common feature of the slip decorated pottery which had not previously been fully realised, but which has been confirmed by this research, is the presence of double-layered white slips. The phenomenon of double-layered slips would appear to be an established part of the decorative technology. A double slip provides a better quality finish (**32**).

The slips were painted onto the vessels to form a variety of highly conventionalised decorative motifs. Over a hundred distinctive designs have been documented. Essentially the motifs can be described as curvilinear, rectilinear, geometric, zoomorphic, complex bands and simple bands. The variety of the motifs, from simple to complex, and the fragmentary nature of much of the material have frustrated attempts to provide a definitive categorisation of the motifs and, inevitably, there are combinations of all the broad categories of

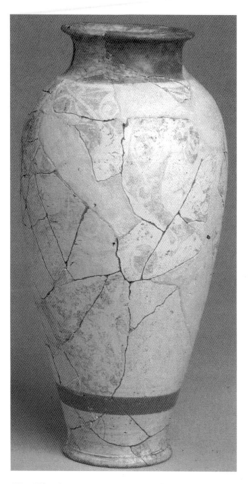

1 cm

30 *The Auvergnian Finewares.* Above and top right: *slip decorated vase and sherd detail;* bottom right: *black burnished ware. Analysis revealed these contrasting wares shared similar coating techniques*

motif described within the assemblage. This case study concerns the technology of decoration involved in the production of bright, paper white vessels on which zoomorphic and geometric designs had been painted in grey paint.

Such fineware has a long chronological presence, early Halstatt examples are known whilst at Aulnat, in common with other European Iron Age sites, this ware is recovered from early-to-late La Tène. Slip-decorated pottery is remarkably uniform across the main European continent. The only major difference to be detected by art-historical studies would be the distribution of zoomorphic patterns which are common in western Atlantic Europe including central France, but are almost completely absent from eastern European contexts. Slip-decorated pottery represents a comparatively rare component of Iron Age pottery assemblages. Figures as low as 0.5 per cent of the assemblage are known from central Europe. For Aulnat, the slip-decorated pottery represent *c.*20 per cent of the overall pottery assemblage and, as such, is a large collection.

Production technology has been assumed to involve updraft kilns with good control over firing atmospheres and uniformity of temperature, in order to achieve the contrasting colour effects of the different-coloured coatings.

Methods of analysis

The analytical challenge for all the pottery investigated was the nature of finewares and their decoration. In areas such as the Auvergne where the clays are fine and homogeneous, body fabric and inclusion study, although helpful, are unlikely to provide answers to questions concerning the technical relationships between the various fineware ceramic types. Archaeometric research has to be focused onto the nature of the decorative coatings themselves. The decorative coatings are extremely thin so that the best way of analyzing them is to take cross

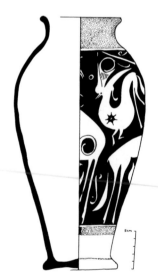

31 *Unicorn design vase*

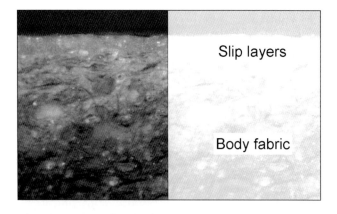

Slip layers

Body fabric

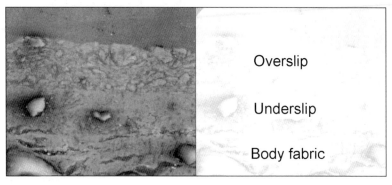

Overslip

Underslip

Body fabric

32 Double-layered slip. Top diagram shows a polished section micrograph of slip-decorated sherd; Below is a SEM micrograph showing composite slip. EDS analysis revealed distinct compositions

sections of sherds and, with the help of reflected light microscopy which shows the contrast of coloured-slip layers of polished sections, plan analysis of the microstructure of the coatings with SEM-EDS. X-ray spot analysis allowed the contrasting chemical composition of the coatings to be examined. The SEM also provides for a detailed examination of the morphology of the ceramic microstructure and relationship of the body fabric to the decorative coating. Powder samples of the surfaces were also removed for X-ray diffraction analysis. XRD studies allow some aspects of resource identification, pigment structure and firing regime to be modelled as various mineral structures can be identified using this technique. A series of re-firing experiments on sherds also allowed investigation of the thermal behaviour of the coatings.

Summary of results for the analysis of slip-decorated pottery
EDS spot analyses of polished cross-sections of the sherds showed that they were of contrasting chemical composition. Figure **32** shows the distinction between the two slip layers and the body fabric of a double-coated ceramic. The bright white outer-slip has a fine particulate structure with interconnecting pores. Below this,

lies the cream-coloured under-slip which has a more closed structure and contains fine aplastic inclusions. The body fabric can be seen underlying the double-slip structure. It has an open porous structure contrasting with the layers above and also contains large, irregular aplastic inclusions (quartz and feldspars). Figure **33** also shows that the slip/slip interface and the slip/body interface are intimate, the slips being very well adhered to each other and to the body fabric. EDS analysis revealed compositional variation among the different slips and body fabrics.

Cream coatings are characterised by their higher content of calcium (see **34**). The bright-white coatings have a low content of iron, calcium and potassium. They also have markedly higher concentration for aluminium when compared to the body fabrics. The aluminium content can be taken as an indicator of clay content and this particular result, along with the low values of iron, potassium and calcium for the coatings may suggest a higher concentration of pure clay minerals in the coatings, such as white kaolin.

The most notable contrast between the under-slip and the body fabric and the other colour groups, is the high content of calcium. The calcium content of all body fabrics is below 5 per cent which represents the use of non-calcareous clays for the slip-decorated pottery. The cream coatings can be seen to contain less iron than the body fabrics, although not as low as the bright-white coatings. These results can be interpreted as the deliberate addition of calcareous materials into the slip preparations to counter the production of red pigments which are normally formed by the oxidation of iron compounds on firing. Calcium suppresses the formation of iron oxides since any iron present in the slip will form calcium iron silicates which are not red in colour.

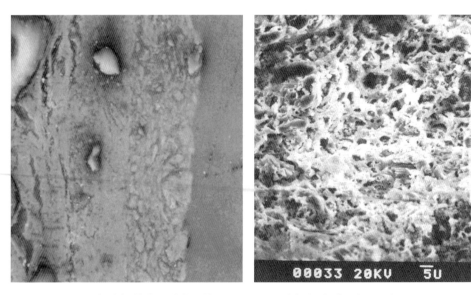

33 *SEM micrograph of double-layered slip. The open structure of the kaolin-based outer slip is seen at higher magnification on the right*

Al	Si	Ca	Fe
32.7	55.2	3.7	2.2

Al	Si	Ca	Fe
14.2	56.7	17.7	4.5

Al	Si	Ca	Fe
19.8	55.6	3.7	11.6

Kaolin bright white overslip (High Al, low Fe)

Calcareous underslip with few inclusions

Iron rich body fabric

34 *Schematic results of EDS spot analysis. Above are typical results, below, the interpretation*

X-ray studies

The X-ray diffractograms of the slips and body fabrics showed the same basic patterns with peaks for illite, muscovite, quartz and feldspar being common to both (**35**). The relative intensities for each were different, the slips having lower feldspar content than the body fabrics and, in some cases, the peaks for the feldspars were missing. This indicates that the slips were made from the fine particle fraction of the body clay.

Consistently, there is relatively less quartz in the slips. These general features of the diffractograms suggest that the coarser rocky particles from the source clays were removed in the process of slip preparation. This could be achieved by elutriation or levigation. The reduced peaks for quartz and feldspars in the slip coatings and the fact that fine quartz particles were observed in the slips macroscopically would suggest that the remaining particles were further reduced by grinding the slip preparation.

The X-ray diffractograms also showed the major unaltered clay mineral detected to be illite. The illite peaks are relatively small and perhaps represent relic peaks from partially destroyed mineral structures caused by their decay on firing, or partially re-hydrated minerals which had been totally de-hydroxylised during the firing process. Illite, when heated above $c.1000°C$, matures to the high temperature mineral phase of mullite. The mullite phase was searched for but not recorded for the XRD results of the slip-decorated pottery. This suggests that the firing temperature was below the threshold of mullite formation.

The XRD results, when considered with the EDS results are consistent with the hypothesis that calcium in the form of calcium carbonates, such as calcined limestones, was added to ferruginous clay slips in order to suppress the formation of red iron oxides and to form calcium iron silicates which are light in colour and thus produce a cream coloured slip.

X-Ray Diffraction analysis

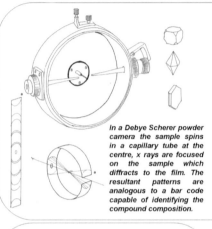

In a Debye Scherer powder camera the sample spins in a capillary tube at the centre, x rays are focused on the sample which diffracts to the film. The resultant patterns are analogous to a bar code capable of identifying the compound composition.

Technique

XRD is a method for identifying and quantifying minerals which have characteristic crystalline structures. These diffract X-rays in specific patterns. When X-rays are shone through a sample, the atoms of the crystal diffract the rays at an angle that depends on the interatomic distances of the lattice. Results are used to calculate the sets of interatomic d values (distances) and compared to known patterns. The method can detect species if they are present in amounts greater than 5% for a diffractometer or 0.1% for a powder camera.

Sampling

Anything crystalline can be sampled. For the powder camera very small amounts of sample are scraped from artefact surfaces or powdered samples removed by cutting or drilling. The sample is then placed in a glass capillary tube and centred in the camera. Sampling for the automated diffractometer involves slightly more sample and is pressed into 35mm aluminium sample holders. Small amounts of sample can be mixed with known substrates to bulk them out and allow them to be pressed into holders. Samples must be prepared carefully to avoid orientation errors where one aspect of the crystal is over-represented. For powder cameras sample preparation is difficult and time consuming.

Samples of ceramic powder pressed into holders

Applications

XRD is used in technology studies and conservation of artefacts. It supplements chemical analysis by providing structural compound information.

Pigments can be identified by XRD. Minerals can also help unravel aspects such as firing temperatures as different minerals are destroyed or begin to form at particular temperatures.

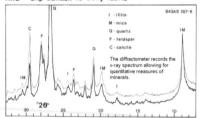

XRD   Slip-burnish vs Body fabric

I - illite
M - mica
Q - quartz
F - feldspar
C - calcite

The diffractometer records the x-ray spectrum allowing for quantitative measures of minerals.

The example of diffractogram above shows the similarity of mineral content for pottery body fabrics and decoration this has important implications in unravelling the sequences of production as a slip of the same clay composition as the body fabric is implied.

35   The principles of X-ray diffraction

Re-firing studies

Re-firing experiments were carried out to ascertain the slip's tolerance to different firing temperatures. This gave an insight into the degree of control with which the ancient kilns were operated.

The bright white slips were notable in that their colour balance did not alter, they maintained their colour throughout the experiment. The cream under-slips had a tendency to darken in colour at higher temperatures and become tinged with red. This may be caused by the maturation of haematite pigments at higher temperatures. This can be seen as a modification of colour balance which was not originally intended by the potters. We have seen how the deliberate addition of calcium to the cream-coloured slips was used as a means of suppressing the formation of red pigments. Control of firing temperatures would, then, appear to be necessary in the production of the cream slips. Observation of colour change to the cream slips can be taken as an indicator of the passing of the original firing temperature. Again such modifications occurred at the higher temperature range (largely above 950°C).

From analytical results to modes of production

The EDS and XRD results have been effective in helping to establish the ways in which the slips were prepared and to reveal the physicochemical relationships which played a part in their colour balance. Concentrations of iron in sherd fabrics have been known to cast a slight cream or pink colour to white slip decorations. The EDS results for the slip-decorated pottery show that the body fabric clays contain over 10 per cent iron oxides. Iron oxides present over 3 per cent in clay will cause a red colour if fired in an oxidising atmosphere. It must be considered, however, that the total amount of iron contained within the body fabric may include nodules of iron-bearing minerals rather than the iron being evenly distributed as fine particulate matter. The distribution of iron within the ceramic, whether it is intimately associated with iron-bearing minerals or present as free oxides within the silicate matrix, will affect the colour contribution of the clay's iron content as a whole.

The addition of calcium for the general recipe of the cream slips also has a technological advantage, together with the noted role in achieving desired colour balance. A calcareous component acts as a flux allowing sintering at lower temperatures. This contributes to the generally well-adhered nature of the cream slip and may have enhanced its role as an under-slip, as well as its role as a primary decorative coating. The cream slips were often observed to have a lustrous quality which could not always be attributed to burnishing by the observation of burnishing facets. It is probable that the high calcium content allowed sintering to achieve the lustre on some of the cream slips.

The phenomenon of cream under-slips for bright-white coatings represents a deliberate attempt to counter the staining power of iron oxides present in body fabrics, which could contribute toward an unwanted colour balance for

RAW MATERIAL

PROCUREMENT
Clay for body and
self-slips
Slip clays (e.g. bright
whites)
Procured pigments (calcium carbonates for creams)
(ocherous materials for reds)
(carbon paint preparations for greys)
N.B. unprocured pigments develop during firing,
they are not added to slip preparations, therefore
procurement of appropriate source clays essential.
Fuel

PROCESSING	BODY FABRIC	SLIP CLAYS
	Drying	Levigation and/or elutriation
	Grinding	Deflocculation
	Sieving/settling	Slip preparation including grinding
	Levigation (fine fraction	and addition of procured pigments
	used for self slips)	(?repeat of all or some of the above
		processes)
	Evaporation	N.B. procured pigments may require
	kneading	processing such as calcining of limestone

TECHNOLOGY

Primary forming
Throwing

Secondary forming
Turning/shaping
Surface preparation
Drying to leather hard state

Surface treatment (variable)

Decoration	STAGE 1	
	Ground or basal slip (self-slip)	Dipping/painting/drying/burnishing
	STAGE 2	
	Red and/or white/cream slip	Dipping/painting/drying/burnishing
	STAGE 3	
	Painting on bands	?marking out designs/painting/
		drying/selective burnishing

Additional processes
Selective and pattern burnishing
Incising

Drying/?preheating

First firing	Kiln loading and fuel preparation	Monitoring and control of the
(for some vessels the only one)		firing process

Post-firing decoration	STAGE 4	
	Zoomorphic, geometric design	Marking/incising (?wax resist)
	painting with carbon paints	painting

Secondary heating
to form amorphous
carbon pigments
(For some designs, may have been more than one re-heating episode)

36   *Suggested model of the sequence of production for slip decorated pottery, based on analytical results*

RAW MATERIAL	LABOUR	TECHNOLOGY	OUTPUT
PROCUREMENT			
Body fabric source clay	Specialist knowledge	Transport, local and	Unprocessed
Slip source clays	(for sources of pigments	long distance	materials
Inorganic pigments	clays and fuel types)		
Deflocculant (?potash)	Unskilled labour		
Carbon pigment precursors			
Water			
Fuel			
PROCESSING			
Drying/crushing	Unskilled labour	Drying sheds/area	Prepared slips
Sieving/settling		Crushing equipment/	(self-slips)
Levigation and/or elutriation	Semi-skilled labour	area, settling/levigation	
of body clays and slip clays		tanks or vessels	Pigmented
Calcining and grinding of		Calcining ovens/	slips
calcium carbonate pigment		fires, grinding and	
Addition and mixing of prepared	Specialist knowledge	sieving equipment for	
pigments e.g. ochres	skilled labour	pigment mixing	
Preparation of amorphous carbon		and storage	
based soot paints			
Drying/crushing	Semi-skilled and	Largely as above	Prepared
Sieving/settling	unskilled labour		body clays
Levigation, evaporation			
and kneading of body clays			
FORMING			
Throwing	Skilled labour	Kick wheel	Semi-finished
Turning/surface preparation			vessels
Surface treatments ground			
(basal) slipping	Skilled labour	Turntable, brushes	
		dipping tanks/vessels	
Drying	Unskilled (storage of	Drying area (?sheds)	Leather hard
	prepared vessels		semi-decorated
Secondary painting of	Skilled labour	Turntable, brushes	vessels
simple and complex bands		marking and burnishing	
Drying	(see above)	tools	
General, selective and pattern			Semi and fully
burnishing			decoratd
			vessels
Firing	Skilled labour	Kiln	Fired vessels
			(some finished)
Post-firing carbon painting	Skilled (?peripatetic	Brushes	
of zoomorphic, curvilinear	artists)	(wax resist?)	fully decorated
and geometric designs			vessels
Secondary heating	Skilled	Smokeless fire or oven	Finished vessels

the bright-white slips. We have already discussed the advantages of calcium-rich slips in suppressing the formation of haematite pigments. This would seem to be a well-understood (albeit in empirical terms) quality which was fully employed by the Auvergnian potters. The phenomenon of double-layered slips represents a sophisticated use of an under-coating technique to produce bright whites. The contrast of the bright-white slips with the greys and reds probably gave the pots a gaudy, bright appearance when new, the untainted 'paper' white composite slip being vital for design impact.

An important aspect of slip preparation obviously was the addition and mixing, where necessary, of processed pigments. The self-slip was also produced, probably from the processing steps involved in treating the fabric clays. For finewares such as those represented in this study, the clays would have been processed by drying, sieving and grinding, to achieve the desired consistency.

Following primary and secondary forming on the wheel, the pots were dried to a leather hard state prior to the application of the prepared slips. The pots were then fired, probably within a kiln where uniform conditions are more likely to enhance appearance of the coating as the fuel is separated from the vessel which is less prone to smudging than is the case for bonfires. Nevertheless, ethnographic situations have noted colourwares being success-fully bonfired and the general lack of evidence for kilns may suggest that bonfiring could have been an alternative means of firing the pottery. The final stage of decoration (stage 4 of **36**) involved the use of carbon paint. Without exception, grey designs disappeared during the re-firing experiments, showing conclusively that they are a post-fire application of carbon-black paint.

The paint is applied to the ceramic and reheated over the smokeless white ash embers of a bonfire. The organic element of the paint chars in the heating process and forms the amorphous carbon-black pigment. The presence of thin painted 'guide lines' on the Auvergnian wares would suggest that this process may have involved many reheating episodes. There is some evidence for the use of a wax-resistant technique for designing the paintings for the Aulnat pottery in the form of brush-marks which run across the long axes of painted designs, rather than along the axes. This perhaps indicates that the brush was used to wash over a resistant design.

On the basis of this reconstruction of the sequence of production, some aspects of the archaeologically invisible variables can be modelled using the components of the production process. A suggested model for the mode of slip-decorated pottery production can be seen in **36**. The production process, from pro-curement of the raw materials, their processing and formation into the finished vessels (output) are modelled together with the likely labour requirements (in terms of specialist knowledge required) and the technology employed.

The production of quality slips would require settling tanks or vessels. Grinding and sieving equipment are also implied together with storage facilities to prevent the contamination of the pure white clays used for the bright-white coatings. Construction and maintenance of a developed kiln in which the gaseous firing conditions, as well as temperature, could be controlled is also inferred. A kick wheel is implied, together with other specialist equipment, most obviously brushes for the painting of designs.

The application of archaeometric information to theoretical frameworks has strengthened and expanded the scope of archaeological inferences concerning the degree of specialisation and labour investment involved in colour-coated ware production in the Auvergne. This case study highlights the importance of using archaeometric analyses to reconstruct modes of production and infer implications to our models of the organisation of production and the nature of craft specialisation.

Conclusions

The two case studies presented here represent contrasting approaches to the study of the organisation of production. One makes use of architectural remains and integrates their analysis with archaeometric data, whilst the other makes use of archaeometric data in the absence of archaeological evidence for production. In the first case study, changes in the way production was organised proved to be a useful means by which to understand changes elsewhere in society. The point that technological change can occur because of non-technical concerns is worth emphasising. A purely archaeometric approach to Alpine copper smelting would not have been able to find meaning in the body of analyses. Only when furnace structures were analysed from an embodied perspective did these results become significant. Such points can thus be considered a call for the practical amalgamation of scientific and archaeological practice.

In the second case study, a more typical situation had given rise to the intervention of archaeometric research. In the absence of direct evidence for pottery production, the analysis aimed to reconstruct the mode of production through considering the sequences of manufacture as evidenced in the microstructural and chemical detail of the products.

Although these case studies have emphasised the organisation of production, the approaches taken can equally address other archaeological themes such as identity and the articulation of power.

4

CRAFT AND CULTURE

Introduction

The greatest contribution of archaeological science to archaeology has been in the fields of dating (see chapter six) and provenance studies (see chapter five). Further contributions have been in the use of physicochemical analysis to the understanding of the technological aspects of ancient production practices. The background to this area of interest and the potential it has to help us understand the varied configurations of craft production and its relationship to our concept of the cultural dimensions of the lives of past people are explored in this chapter. Observations of key concepts such as craft and culture are made and how they are theoretically integrated into our interpretations of past technological practices. This is followed by discussion of a case study that illustrates attempts to involve archaeometric analysis in relevant archaeological questions.

Ideas about action

The acts of making and using things are at the root of much of what we do as human beings. It is the material manifestation of those actions that some archaeometrists study. But the human world is not just about materials and action, it is also about ideas. Some archaeological scientists have celebrated the fact that the physical constants, the objectively defined parameters, such as melting points and chemical reactions with which they deal, connect us to an absolute reality of past action in relation to how things were made in the past. Of course, being able to understand the technical detail of such action is extremely valuable but it is only part of the equation. For instance, it is useful to know that 'grog' (ground-up broken pottery) may be present in pottery as a deliberately added tempering agent. It might also be useful to know that the action of putting the grog into the pottery was technologically beneficial as it helped to open up the fabric to allow potentially destructive pressures of escaping gases to dissipate during firing. Equally, it is valuable to know that the expansion coefficient of the grog is similar to the thermal behaviour of the bulk of the clay into which it has been included. Such knowledge helps us to appreciate the value of the grog as an inclusion that fired in sympathy with the developing ceramic body of which it is a part. But in terms of understanding the technological *choice* of the grog as an inclusion, we need to look to the ideas, belief systems and ways of knowing the world of the potter.

This ideational aspect of production technology involves us with the phenomenon of choice: why grog and not sand, or something else? Of course, in considering these ideas it is important to consider factors beyond the functional, physical and the measurable. But are these ideas to be suppressed in our consideration of past craft production just because of their metaphysical quality? We can observe such choices ethnographically; moreover, their consideration allows us to appreciate wider aspects of material culture and refine the integration of archaeometric research. For example, is it just storage jars that contain grog? How does the distribution of different types of vessel pan out over different components of a settlement system? What exactly might the storage jars have contained? Was grog inclusion an innovation? If so, does it coincide with changes in other aspects of social life, such as change in diet or burial tradition?

The above discussion has highlighted the relationship between archaeological interpretation and archaeological science. Although interrelated, archaeology and archaeometry too often practise as separate entities and need to be consciously integrated for either to be successful in the process of archaeological interpretation. Archaeometry involves the investigation of the objectively measurable parameters of the physical, chemical and biological realities of matter. The facts of matter, chemical composition, microstructure and age are then considered to try to understand how and why humans behaved in particular ways. It is where the integration of fact to an interpretative framework occurs that scientists and archaeologists need to refine their collaboration.

Seeing beyond the obvious

Archaeological science has played a major role in developing and advancing the study of the technical part of technological processes. An important component of this approach is an appreciation of the theoretical foundation to interpretation. These foundations can be characterised by the analogy of a ladder, famously used by Christopher Hawkes: the so-called ladder of inference

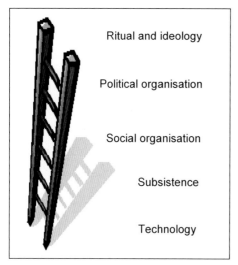

Ritual and ideology

Political organisation

Social organisation

Subsistence

Technology

37 Hawkes' Ladder of Inference

(**37**). This ladder visualised the goals and aspirations of archaeology as a series of rungs or levels, with each becoming more difficult and requiring more complex investigation. At the top the ultimate goal of archaeological endeavour was an understanding of the belief systems, i.e. ritual and religion. Beneath this, were social status and economic aspects of behaviour that still required considerable effort to reach. The easily achieved lower rungs of the ladder were occupied by technology, aspects of production and artefacts.

This view rested on the misguided belief that technology was an obvious set of physical processes divorced from social behaviours or aspects of choice. Research aimed at the technological aspects of production of artefacts was therefore seen as somehow less prestigious or worthy than those research programmes aimed at the top of the ladder. Such a view persisted until relatively recently and may account for the relative lack of integration of theory and practice in the field of archaeometry related to artefact analysis. Recently, the view of the status of technological studies has changed dramatically. The realisation that technology is a fully social phenomenon has invigorated research into many fields of study. However, the integration of archaeometry and theory has only recently began to emerge.

For transformative technologies such as ceramics, glassmaking and metallurgy, where raw materials are mixed, modified and affected by heat (pyrotechnology), the chemical and physical data may be difficult to interpret, but it *is* possible to investigate the production steps and operational sequences involved. Through paying attention to the details of production, more can be revealed about such aspects as specialisation, labour investment, organisation and inroads made into trying to understand those parameters of production that may be associated with the ideas and beliefs held by those involved in transformative technologies. We should also be aware of, and open to, the possible symbolic currencies that may have surrounded those people who turned clay into stone and stone into metals.

What is a culture?

Reflect for just a moment to consider how many objects we use everyday. Buildings, beds, bedclothes, alarm clocks, kettles, taps, containers, cutlery, furniture . . . and that's probably only within the first ten minutes of a typical day. The only things we make ourselves in the above scenario is a coffee and maybe the bed. Whilst it is likely that people in remote pasts were more used to making the everyday things that they used, we should not automatically jump to the conclusion that each individual was a self-sufficient boy-scout or girl-guide. Nevertheless, action within craft-based production was likely to have been a far more prominent and visible aspect of past society than it is in ours and this is simply the reflection of the historical, technological and social configuration in which we currently live that favours mass production and mass consumption. Incidentally, a configuration that is by no means inevitable or, indeed, sustainable.

All the countless objects of human lives and the way we conceive of them and use them within a social context are part of 'culture'. More specifically, the objects themselves are known as 'material culture'. The places that we modify through actions, such as settlement buildings, also form part of our culture. In fact almost everything we conceptualise, name and interact with becomes incorporated into our notion of culture. In this way, almost everything can be regarded as cultural. One extreme to 'cultural' is 'natural' but even here we can establish cultural meaning and identity through ideas or interaction. An elephant for example could be considered 'natural', but if we place it in a zoo, shoot at it, write about it or draw it, the elephant has cultural meaning too, as an exhibit, a resource, as a hunting trophy or as an expression of cultural, for example, poetic or symbolic values. The important point here is that the idea of 'a culture' includes a group's belief system and their attitudes and ideas towards matters such as food production and consumption, appropriate kinship and social relations, appropriate use of space – in short, the entirety of a culture's ways of knowing and living in the world.

We argue here that the actions of production or modification should be the focus of our integration of archaeometric and archaeological study. Understanding exactly how an artefact was produced, rather than simply what it is made of, will help in our understanding of issues central to the cultural conditions surrounding its production. So how can we examine the interplay of craft production and cultural meaning? Through a case study of the manu-facture of pottery, the contribution of archaeometric analyses in revealing the technological aspects of production and what these aspects might reveal about our understanding of cultural meanings of production are explored. Fundamental to this chapter is our argument that it is the study of production, as well as use and consumption, that should be considered more as a primary phase of analysis and study. All too often, consideration of how an artefact was produced has been overlooked by considerations of where it came from and how it was consumed. We wonder, in fact, whether these areas of interest are subconscious reflections of our own cultural conditioning where the origin and consumption of things is something we readily engage with and consider important, while acts of production, now rare within our own cultural environment, tend to be overlooked in our accounts of times past.

Studying culture

Cultural meanings are contingent to a complex web of factors including, but not exclusively, historical circumstance, social, political, economic and ideational circumstances. As we innovate, produce, use and consume objects within a social milieu, their meanings can change. Objects of material culture as produced are pretty much fixed. A plastic pen, for example, is a plastic pen – used for writing for a while, perhaps exchanged – swapped in the school yard maybe. Then used in a fight to poke someone's eye out. Does it mean the pen is now a weapon? Or maybe it is now a carefully labelled and bagged item of evidence in a court case. Maybe it could be used at the roadside as an emergency tracheotomy tube, converted into a pea-shooter, or esteemed as an heirloom because of its association with a momentous treaty signature or touched by a popular idol in signing an autograph. There are in fact countless trajectories or biography's for a pen and fluxing meanings that could be attached to it depending on the historical and social context in which it is considered. The materiality of the object maybe fixed, but its meanings and uses are not.

If we were to consider activities within the 'front' room of a British suburban house built in the 1930s, we would probably discover, over relatively short periods of time in the decades of the later twentieth century, huge fluxes in the sorts of activities and their cultural associations. Such changes result from the complex interplay of social, political, technological, economic, historic and ideational, that is, cultural factors.

Let us imagine some 'deca-peeping'. In the 1950s the room is very neat and tidy but full of interesting artefacts that display the wealth, status and interests of the family, including formal photographs of important, usually dead, family members arranged on the mantelpiece. The furniture is set out formally around the fireplace, but the room is devoid of people. It is used for special occasions only, usually on a Sunday afternoon when guests may need to be entertained. Very rarely it is used to lay-out dead family members as part of funerary rituals. In the 1960s the room is unbelievably untidy, the house has changed ownership and a young and expanding family has moved in. The room is full of an eclectic mix of family games, clothes drying on the newly installed central heating radiators, an ironing board, a record player and furniture, but space has been cleared in the middle as a play area for when the weather is bad. It has become a general family 'living' room. We are now in the 1970s: the room is still a living room but the focus of the room now is the television set, there are also informal photographs of current family members. The fireplace has been blocked off to create more space. It has become a room that is used more in the late afternoon and early evening during broadcasting of television programmes. In the 1980s the room is almost always occupied by some family members watching television; broadcasts are throughout the day and night. It's the 1990s now and there has been a dramatic change. The room is now used as a bedroom. The house has been sold to a landlord who has divided it into flats. The bottom half of the house is now one flat and the 'front' room is now used largely for sleeping. Only one person, a single professional man occupies the entire flat.

The above consideration of the activities and associated artefacts and social use of space within a room illustrates the fluxing interplay of the complex factors that determine what could be termed cultural identity. We could typify some of the characterisations and patterns of artefacts and their uses if we were to compare many front rooms through time. We could perhaps recognise repeated patterns of consistent use and artefact types in the majority of front rooms at different times. Any such patterns recognised could be termed cultural stereotypes. It is the difference from our current cultural stereotype that allows us to recognise others. Over relatively short periods of time, as cultural identities and related behaviours that are part of their creation change, we can generate further culturally conditioned phenomena such as nostalgia. Often these too may result in a recycling of cultural stereotypes as can be seen in the current trend for re-installing fire-places as focal points and stripping out-fitted carpets. These are arguably just elements of fashion but, of course, the phenomenon of fashion is inevitably caught up the complex process of cultural conditioning.

Archaeologists are the peeping Toms, or Tabathas, of time. They study the flux and change of culture over huge areas and over vastly expanded time frames than that considered above. Moreover, they cannot observe the people or their actions; instead, they have to imagine people and infer their actions and how they constructed social relations from the material remains that they left behind. They refer to 'material' culture. As we have seen by the above discussion, material culture is an enormously complex and diverse area of interest, influenced by unpredictable interplay of conditioning factors. Archaeologists also have to consider that the material culture from archaeological sites is just a fraction of evidence, incomplete owing to processes of decomposition and sampling bias.

Let's take an example. Finding pottery in archaeological deposits in Britain is almost expected on the majority of excavations dealing with the last six thousand years or so. Pottery is used today and is recorded from ethnographic observations as storage containers, to serve food, to convey social messages, to display ethnic identities, to cook food, to contain dead people, to contain the souls of the dead, to carry water, to contain evil spirits or benevolent ones, to represent ancestors, to smash at social gatherings, to advertise a commodity or service . . . there is an end to the list, but it is too far away to reach here. The point is that the cultural meaning and use of pottery within particular contexts and in association with other culturally meaningful things is infinite. There is a rich ethnographic record of observations made of present human societies' use of pottery that archaeologists can use as sources of inspiration.

Nigel Barley has drawn together observations relating to pottery production and use in Cameroon. He points out that pottery in some Cameroon societies can be considered as vehicles of cultural meanings, associated with women potters who, through their potting, uphold tradition and cultural conservatism. Metallurgy, on the other hand, is, in those same societies, practiced by men and is associated with innovation. Beyond the mundane uses of pottery, Barley considers aesthetic, gender roles, power relations and models of the human body, the seasons of the year and procreation and reincarnation in ceramic production use and consumption. Most interesting is his assertion that the importance of pots in Cameroon derives from a concern with 'non-material forces' that can only act through localisation in a material object that serves to contain or direct the force.

As one example, pottery production amongst the Dowayo people of Northern Cameroon is considered dangerous. The women potters are capable of causing haemorrhoids in men and deformed vaginas in other women. If a rain chief were to meet a potter or a metal smith, both would die according to Dowayo belief systems. As a result since the rain chief needs pottery to control the rain, complex arrangements are made whereby those at both ends of the social scale are brought together. The arrangements involve post-menopausal potters firing pottery intended for the rain chief on a moonless night in a shelter used to house dead male bodies and passing them on to a sorcerer for transport to the rain chief.

No amount of excavation, archaeometric analysis, theorising and middle-range experimentation could hope to allow archaeologists to recreate the *exact* cultural specifics of Dowayo potting traditions. The important point, however, is that such ethnographic observation allows us to imagine the rich cultural meanings and practices that are possible. There is more to ancient pottery than determining what a pot was used for or its use as a chrono-typological marker. A pot is not simply a pot; it is more a way of life. Of course pots are just one element of material culture and the other elements too have their own complex interplays with determining, shaping and revealing cultural meaning.

So where do we begin? The materiality of the object can be explored. We can weigh it, measure it, conserve it, draw it, photograph it, analyse its chemical make-up, study its physicality through microscopy, determine whether it has residues of other substances adhering to it. These empirical observations born of scientific procedure provide valuable data about the object. But what of its cultural meaning? We have to theorise through comparison with our current understanding about how objects are used and what they may mean to the people who use them and the human stories they may reflect. Analogy with current observations cannot recreate an exact replica of the socio-cultural milieu from which the object originated, but we can use our archaeological imagination to approximate some possibilities to animate our interpretations of a human past. Using archaeometric analysis can also help narrow down certain possibilities, so that our archaeological imaginations do not run riot and emerge into a never-never world of random, 'anything-goes' explanations.

The cult of culture

The idea of a culture as a characteristic way of life developed in the 1750s when German ethnologists began to use 'kultur' as a word to characterise the rural way of life as recognisably different from the 'civilising' effects of urban life. The word 'culture' developed into its broader modern meaning through the work of late-nineteenth century ethnographers who used it to denote a particular form, stage or type of intellectual development or civilisation. By this time, the influence of evolutionary theory had woven into the concept of culture the theme of progression and development through time. Particular groups of people were considered as more or less cultured. Archaeologists and anthropologists debated less-developed cultures evolving towards idealised civilised ones. Culture was related to ideas concerning race where 'primitive' tribes of 'dark-skinned', less intelligent people represented lower forms of culture shot through with taboos and irrational ritual expressions of how the world worked. White people were held as being more intelligent and capable of higher forms of cultural expression through a more rational understanding of how the world works, supposedly evidenced by their literature, science and arts, especially music. Of course, degrees of barbarity were tolerated for those ancient light-skinned tribes that were, after all, busily striving towards the enlightenment that was to be the inheritance of the largely white 'privileged' middle classes that studied them.

Archaeological cultures were inferred from recognisable suites of characteristic objects and settlement patterns, observable spatially as prehistoric territories of cultural influence and temporally through stratigraphy. It was possible therefore to map out particular cultural associations and observe changes through time. The driving forces behind such changes were seen to be diffusion of ideas and invasions of other cultures. This approach was developed initially by Franz Boas and typified by the Australian archaeologist, Gordon Childe. Childe's work in Europe, notably his book *The Dawn of European Civilisation* (1925) and *The Most Ancient Near East* (1928), established him as the leading archaeological theorist of his generation. He had established the culture-history approach in *The Danube In Prehistory* (1929) that employed the hypothesis that distinctive 'packages' of artefacts reflected distinct ethnic groups. Unsupportable assumptions were made that connected material remains of cultural groups with other aspects of culture such as spoken language and religion. Childe's culture-history approach in part formalised work that had been taking shape in Europe through the work of archaeologists such as Gustav Kossina who developed 'settlement archaeology'. Kossina's approach traced back material cultural associations of German-speaking territories to 'demonstrate' that the pristine culture of German-speaking areas had been 'tainted' by invasions of lesser cultures in prehistory. Settlement archaeology was embraced by the Nazi regime which used such concepts as validation for 're-invasions' of those areas that could be shown through material cultural associations to have been Germanic in prehistory and, of course, the heinous policy of rooting out the 'tainting' influences through genocide of 'alien' ethnic cultures.

The experience of the Second World War set the conditions for new attitudes towards the concept of culture. The rise of new archaeology in the 1960s, with its emphasis on 'culture processes', initiated a considerable negativity towards the culture-history approach. Culture process used systems theory to subdivide a culture into component sub-systems, for examples, technological processes, food-getting processes, ritual activities and exchange processes. Ethnography was used to show that the patterns of material remains observable could be related to the processes of how human groups operated. These considerations illustrated that material culture could be usefully read as adaptive responses that were largely determined by environmental factors. Material culture was therefore only incidentally, and not inevitably, associated with ethnic or cultural identity. In fact material culture, in the words of Lewis Binford was seen as an 'extrasomatic means of adaptation to the environment'.

The so-called Mousterian debate is perhaps the clearest illustration of the difference between the culture process approach and the culture-history approach. Francois Bordes, an expert in middle Palaeolithic (Mousterian) flint tools, had read the vertical stratigraphy of recognisably different tools as the record through time of successive culture histories. That is through time, different cultural groupings of Neanderthals had occupied different areas, depositing their cultural identity in the form of recognisably different sets of stone tools. Lewis Binford criticised the culture-historical approach to the archaeological record. He suggested, from his experience of observing hunter groups in the arctic, that the same group of people left behind a recognisably different collection of stone tools depending on the tasks that they were undertaking and that those tasks were largely seasonally differentiated. Binford suggested that Bordes was wrong in picturing several Neanderthal cultures. It was likely one group, but several cultural processes represented by the stone tool assemblage.

On the face of it, there was no way of verifying either story. Binford, however, had championed a scientific methodology that he termed 'middle range theory' and experimentation. By examining the use-ware patterns of stone tool edges and through a scientifically rigorous programme of blind tests and control experimentation conducted on modern replicates, Binford connected the 'static' record of stone tool assemblages to the 'dynamics' of cultural processes in the past. He proved his point through scientific observation and middle range theory ('middle' describes the space between the dynamics of the past and the static record of the present).

As this new archaeology was embraced and further developed, the role of science and ethnography became firmly established in the investigation of how past peoples 'functioned'. Cultural change was seen as a process that was explained in terms of systems theory. Culture-history has re-emerged in the late twentieth century as a viable research paradigm, following its demise in the mid-twentieth century as 'new' or 'processual' approaches turned the spotlight of investigation away from cultural groups to the uncovering of general laws of human behaviour. The hiatus of the culture-history approach in the period between the 1960s and the 1990s, through which processual archaeology emerged, was of critical importance to archaeology.

The dominance of processual archaeology in the 1970s galvanised the scientification of archaeology and helped to establish scientistic methodologies. The new scientific approaches, at the same time, neutralised archaeological explanation in terms of individuals in the past. Cultural traits, the ethnicity that coloured the lives of past people and enlivened our imaginations of them, became demonised by new archaeology as a kind of obscuring smoke-screen that covered the scientific truth of general laws of human behaviour. Processual archaeology failed to turn the discipline into a science through the wilting criticism of archaeologists who recognised the value of new scientific methodologies but, at the same time, realised the paucity of explanations that ignored the historical and cultural nature of human society.

Breathing life into artefact studies

Presently, there is a tendency to embrace aspects of processual and historical aspects of archaeological interpretation. Some have referred to this combination as the 'cognitive-processual' approach. We should perhaps aim to encourage research that addresses the social and experiential aspects of ancient production processes through a multi-disciplinary approach to study materials science, experiential archaeology and socio-cultural theory. The development of a synthesis between science and material-culture studies will mark, in our opinion, a new phase of technological studies. We see a trajectory which takes us beyond study of materials within positivist networks and through interpretative models of social organisation as reflected throughout the production sequences to those which allow us to address the experiential nature of pyrotechnologies – the sweat, tears, boredom, excitement, smells and tastes of the process which turned raw materials into useful things.

We have given some of the flavour of the various debates that have revolved around the field of interests related to ancient production processes. There is an element of circularity to the trends of analysis and research questions that have been addressed. Ironically, the tendency to treat objects as if they were living, breathing entities has, to a certain extent, resurfaced as elements of the culture-history approach are recycled. Ideas relating to the biography of artefacts have come from social theorists examining the social life of things whilst trying to understand how and why people chose to make things in particular ways. Such approaches invite archaeometric engagement not least since they converge, albeit awkwardly, with ideas of material and artefact life-cycles.

The biographical approach to studying ancient artefacts could integrate the archaeometric with archaeological approaches to interpretation. In this approach the stages and choices involved in creating an artefact are considered in order to unravel the sequence of technological and ideational events in the life-history of a particular object, from the procurement of raw materials, through the craft production stages, to artefact use/reuse and eventual discard. This approach has been linked to the key methodological and theoretical concept of the *chaîne opératoire*. The *chaîne opératoire* (operational sequence) concept originates from the work of Marcel Mauss further developed by Leroi-Gourhan (see chapter seven).

We react to objects as we excavate, measure, analyse and conserve them. Our experience of them is the latest stage in the cultural biography of those artefacts as we interpret them. The concept of artefact biography, *chaîne opératoire* and life-cycle forces the archaeometrist and archaeologist alike to recognise the social context of technological processes through the creation, use and deposition of artefacts. The current interest in biographies can be related to the development of an 'anthropology of technology'. The anthropological approach has revitalised the study of ancient technological processes and recognises their social and ideational contexts.

Case study: Neolithic pottery on the Isle of Man

Introduction

This case study refers to a particular type of Neolithic pot excavated from the Billown Quarry Site, Isle of Man (see chapter two). The assemblage of these so-called earthfast jars (**38**) offers an interesting avenue of research when considering pottery life-cycles. Earthfast jars were deliberately buried unbroken so that their rims were level with the subsoil and were sometimes topped with a removable lid, usually of slate (**39**), and often in the proximity of cremation cemeteries. This deposition contrasts strongly with the remainder of Manx ceramic assemblages, which are highly fragmented. Thus earthfast jar deposition which, with other pottery, would equate with breakage and discard, can be argued to represent the use of the jars, or the beginning of another phase in the

38   Above and below: *The earthfast jars excavated from the Billown Quarry site.* Photos: Tim Darvill

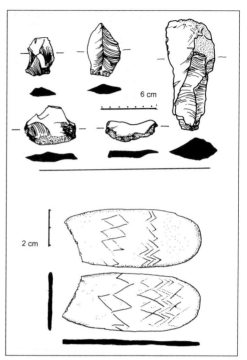

39 Above: *Earthfast jar with slate lid.*
Photograph: Tim Darvill

40 Right: *Illustration of Ronaldsway material culture.* Redrawn from Cubbon

earthfast jar's cultural biography. The unusual burial context of earthfast jars poses interesting questions about their possible functions and provides an opportunity to consider an atypical 'end' to a life-cycle analysis of pottery.

Archaeological Background

Earthfast jars are attributed to the Ronaldsway Culture of the Isle of Man which is a clearly discernible and geographically focused late-Neolithic grouping spanning the third millennium BC. The major features of the Ronaldsway material culture were: stone axes with roughened butts, engraved stone plaques, thick hump-backed scrapers, polished flint knives, hollow scrapers, lozenge shaped arrow-heads and deep baggy ceramic jars with overhanging rims (**40**).

Excavations as part of the Billown Neolithic Landscape Project under the direction of Prof. Tim Darvill have so far produced four earthfast jars. One of the jars (**41**) has a series of dark-coloured bands and chevrons on the outer surface that became more apparent following restoration. Banding and fire-clouding is more prevalent on earthfast jars than other classes of Manx Neolithic pottery. However, it should be noted that it may be more readily recognised on the earthfast jars as they recovered as whole vessels by virtue of their depositional context. It is more difficult to observe such features on single sherds of other pottery. It has been suggested that the banding and fire-clouding patterns observable on earthfast jars may be related to the firing process and relate to

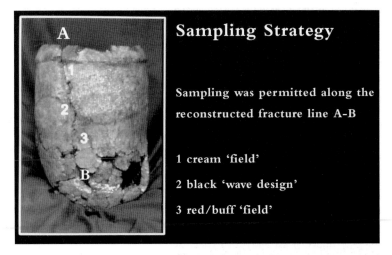

Sampling Strategy

Sampling was permitted along the reconstructed fracture line A-B

1 cream 'field'

2 black 'wave design'

3 red/buff 'field'

41 *Earthfast jar showing fields of decoration*

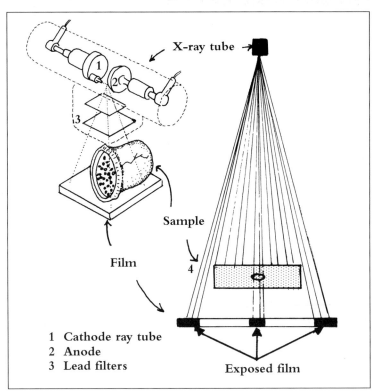

X-ray tube

Sample

Film

1 Cathode ray tube
2 Anode
3 Lead filters

Exposed film

42 *Diagram of how X-radiography works*

decorative function. If deliberate, the 'design' would also represent one of the earliest examples of painted pottery in northwestern Europe.

A programme of analytical work was undertaken to ascertain whether the apparent patterning on the jar was post-depositional or a deliberately manufactured aspect of the pot. Key questions asked whether coloured slips were used to decorate the surfaces of the jar. In particular, was the black chevron carbon related to fire-clouding or an iron-rich reduced slip? The use context of the buried jar would make any decoration unobservable from the surface but earlier uses may have been important before the vessel was selected for use in this way. Also of importance is the significance of colour and decoration to the people in the Neolithic. The possible decoration is of course also of importance to any analysis of operational sequences and their relationship to matters such as 'style' and social expression.

Investigative procedure

Prior to taking samples from the pot, it was photographed and subjected to X-radiography. X-radiography (**42**) uses x-rays to expose internal structure that can assist in identifying the means of production. Such investigation found that the vessel had been coil built, probably in two sections (base and body) with the neck having been pulled-up to an extent, as also evidenced by finger-tip striations remaining on the interior of the vessel. It was also revealed that the rim of the pot had been added as a separate grit-free component and not particularly well keyed into the rest of the pot (**43**). This observation echoes those made on other earthfast jars, where sooting has been observed on small extant cracks between the body and the rim.

Small samples were removed from areas of the jar where different fields of colour could be observed. Optical microscopy of these samples revealed that a slip layer had been applied to the surface to give it a grit-free appearance which contrasted with the inclusion-rich body fabric (**44**). Although cracked, the

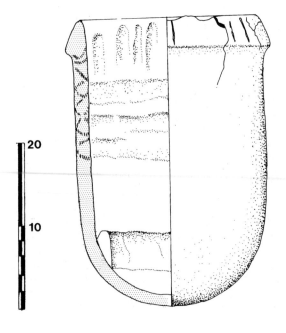

43 *Earthfast jar showing internal structure as revealed by X-radiography prior to excavation of the soil fill.* Redrawn from Darvill, 2001

44 *Cracked surface of earthfast jar showing decorative coating*

45 *Photomicrograph showing distinction between slip and body fabric*

46 *Photomicrograph (SEM) of slip layer on earthfast jar*

surface (**45**) only exhibits occasional spalling from protruding inclusions, generally it is well adhered, suggesting that the slurry was composed of levigated fractions of the same clay as the body. Such good adhesion can be attributed to similar thermal properties of slip and body fabric. A clear distinction between the surface slip and the body fabric can be seen in **46**.

The samples examined using optical microscopy were also used for SEM-EDS analysis (**16**). Individual clay particles could be resolved which were largely thermally unmodified. Determining the degree of vitrification allows estimates to be made for the firing temperature; it appeared that a low-temperature firing regime was employed such as a bonfire.

The sample from the apparently black painted chevron around half the circumference of the pot was analysed using the X-ray energy dispersive spectrometer (EDS) on the SEM. It was important to ascertain whether the black pigment was carbon or iron. SEM-EDS would not normally be considered useful for identifying carbon deposits but within the scope of this question and having optimised the instrument, results proved fruitful. The sample was not coated to reduce static in the SEM-EDS and for the black surface a carbon peak was detected whilst it was absent from non-black samples (**47**). The black-surface sample was then fired in an oxidising atmosphere at 500°C for fifteen minutes with the intention of burning off the carbon. Results showed a loss of black colouration and a reversion to body fabric colour. It was

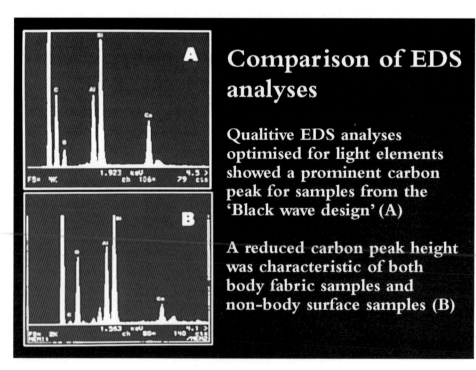

Comparison of EDS analyses

Qualitive EDS analyses optimised for light elements showed a prominent carbon peak for samples from the 'Black wave design' (A)

A reduced carbon peak height was characteristic of both body fabric samples and non-body surface samples (B)

47   *EDS spectrum showing absence of carbon peak on refired black-painted sample*

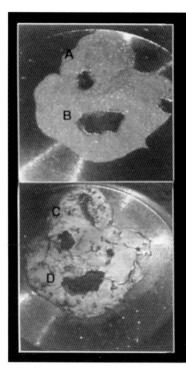

Re-firing experiments

Samples of the 'black wave design' surface coating were fired in an oxidising atmosphere at 500°C with a soak time of 15 minutes

Results showed a loss of black colouration and reversion to body fabric colour

- surface prior to re-firing
- body fabric prior to re-firing
- surface after re-firing
- body fabric after re-firing

48 *Re-firing experiments*

presumed that, if the colour was due to carbon, then no carbon would now be detected whereas, if it was iron, then an iron peak would still be present. Re-analysis by SEM-EDS clearly showed an absence of the carbon peak and limited iron peak suggesting that the black colour was the result of carbon pigmentation (**48**). The black wave design then results from the application of a carbon-based medium, or perhaps infused carbon resulting from fire-clouding. The uniformity of the wave pattern suggests that this is a deliberate design. Rubbing organic matter or liquid over the vessel surface and subsequently heating to carbonise the design or indeed executing the design whilst the vessel was still hot following its firing may have been possible techniques.

Observations made during consolidation and restoration of earthfast jars suggest that some of the pots, whilst having robust rims and shoulders, do not have well preserved bases; indeed they could in some cases be described as severely under-fired. This would tie in with the suggestion that these pots were fired partly buried with incomplete maturation of ceramic phases in those parts not fully exposed to the heat of the fire. This might suggest that the pot makers were not overly concerned with properties relating to storage and durability.

Widening fields of analysis
The sampling methodology adopted here was a direct response to the question of intentionality concerning decorative operations. Specific techniques were

chosen in the analysis at the expense of others to answer the question posed. Blind archaeometric analysis would not have created data that could necessarily address these questions. Here we have considered just a couple of moments in the overall biography of this artefact. The cultural biographic approach demands appraising archaeometric results within its archaeological, symbolic and artistic context in order to move towards a better understanding of its creation and use, thus avoiding another 'so-what story' from an archaeometrist.

When considering the life-cycle of the earthfast jars, we should be aware of the possible symbolic currencies that these pots held. In addressing these possibilities we have to examine the circumstances of deposition across the island. As often in archaeology we are dealing with a fragmented and incomplete record of chance finds and often poorly recorded excavations. Nevertheless we can glean some useful observations from the evidence available:

- Morphologically there appears to be a distinction between taller straighter jars and squatter more rounded examples.
- The contents of the jars vary from empty to containing sherds of other vessels, bone pins, rarely cremated human bone and organic residues.
- The capstones are often very effective at sealing the jars suggesting they were associated with the manufacture of the jar.
- Banding colour effects and incised rim decoration appear to be important for some of the jars.
- The jars are sometimes found in association with white quartz beach pebbles and close to cremation deposits and burnt areas that have been interpreted as the remains of funeral pyres.

Three sites stand out in the quality of evidence that allows a clearer picture of the nature of deposition of some of the earthfast jars, namely Ballateare, Killeaba and Billown Quarry Site (**49**). Tim Darvill points out from the evidence at Billown Quarry Site that it is unlikely that such jars were isolated and forgotten features. Four jars have been recovered to date from this site (**50**). Two lay immediately west of a circular enclosure, one being partly surrounded by a shallow gully. A third was discovered two metres to the south surrounded by a series of large post holes. These jars and the post holes and gullies associated with them lie on a levelled platform cut into the hill slope to form what Darvill interprets as a recurrent focus of attention. A shallow scoop on the platform contained a grey clay layer that appeared to have been formed into a bowl shape with evidence of burning and bone. The whole site was scattered with white quartz beach pebbles and leaf-shaped arrow-heads. A fourth earthfast jar in a state of poor preservation was uncovered 20m to the south of the other three, on the outside of a major Neolithic boundary ditch.

Similar evidence was found at Ballateare where it seems jars may have been set against a wooden fence. Six jars were grouped at Ballateare associated with

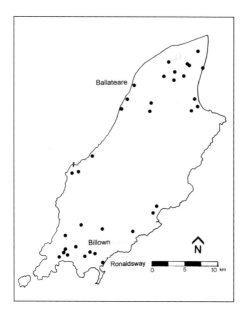

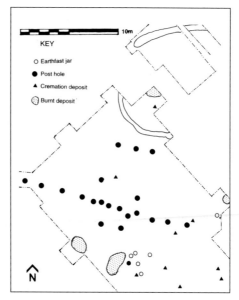

49 Above: *Map of Isle of Man showing location of Ballateare (left) and plan showing distribution of earthfast jars referred at Ballateare (right)*

50 Right: *Distribution of earthfast jars at the Billown Quarry site.* Redrawn from Darvill, 1997

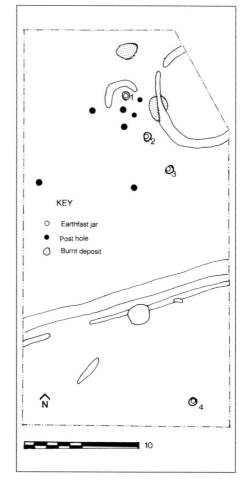

a series of scoops containing cremation deposits. Although damaged by later agricultural activities, the jars had been carefully set in pits, some with stones set in the bottom of the pits to ensure their upright position. Again there was evidence for slate capstones. The jars were associated with cremation deposits that were discovered in a layer corresponding to the upper parts of the earthfast jars. The dense deposits of cremated bone suggested to the excavator Gerhard Bersu that each cremation had been packed into a container such as a hide bag. One of the better-preserved jars was interred in an elongated pit and had either slumped or had been deliberately placed on its side. This jar contained cremated bone and a smaller jar in which were more cremated bones, a pig-bone pin fragment and a polished flint knife. The site is interpreted as a cemetery complex in which groups of earthfast jars were placed amongst cremation burials and, in one case, was the depository for a burial. Four shallow scoops of dark earth containing charcoal, ash and burnt bone and pottery are thought to be the remains of cremation pyres. Arrangements of post holes occur across the site which had been lined with beach stones. The post holes probably represent screen fences that may have been contemporary with the cemetery.

At the site of Killeaba, on a natural mound, a burning pit was discovered just south of the mound's summit as well as four timber-lined pits, one of which contained a cremation burial interpreted as having been contained in a skin bag. Six cremation burials were recovered in the form of dense pockets of cremated bone reminiscent of Ballateare. One originally slate-capped earthfast jar occupied the summit of the mound just above the burning pit, whilst another was found associated with one of the timber lined pits without a lid.

Knocksharry is another natural mound site with jars and evidence of cremation. Jars, cobbled platforms and burning pits were revealed by excavation. However the level of recording of these features was poor and the ceramic assemblage was poorly restored.

Were these pots specifically made for ritual deposition, or did they have a phase in their cultural biography where they were in use before deposition? The fact that of all pots recovered there are a number of examples which have remained intact and often empty, save for the accumulation of silts, would suggest that the cap-stones were part of the pot. It is possible therefore that some of these pots were specifically created for deposition within carefully chosen and prepared sites.

The manner in which these pots were made and, equally importantly, used defines a style unique to the Isle of Man. The gestures, which animated the building, firing and use of these pots can in part be recovered. The chain of production and use sequences that culminated in the incorporation of earthfast jars into the archaeological record, produce the *isochrestic* element of style. The open firing of the pots produced a high incidence of fire-clouding forming bands and chevrons, which may have echoed designs used elsewhere in the Manx Neolithic. The reinforcement of the patterns observed following firing or, indeed, applied whilst the vessel was still within its smouldering bonfire, would entail the *iconological* reinforcement of style, a more deliberate application to reinforce ethnic or group meaning. Such assertions are made possible by archaeometric analyses that show decoration was certainly intentional.

If we consider transformative technologies ethnographically there is a bewildering array of human diversity in the acting out of production processes and products often invoking social metaphors for human reproduction. Perhaps some of the vessels were considered to be 'marked' in some way and singled out for special treatment. But why bother to decorate a pot or appreciate its fire-clouding pattern as special and then insert it into the ground? Here observations of the distribution of well-recognised decorative motifs from rock art and grooved-ware pottery may be relevant. Carved designs at passage tombs in the Boyne Valley are placed in different locations that may reflect changing social access to designs whilst grooved-ware pots with specific designs were often buried at strategic locations to emphasise their importance.

Can we speak of the earthfast jars as symbolic people or perhaps symbolic tombs? Cremation burials mark the funerary rite of the later Neolithic on the Isle of Man, contrasting with long barrows and passage graves of the middle Neolithic which, nevertheless, often contained cremated remains. The tomb represents a location for the dead that is accessible and can be re-entered. The removable lids of the earthfast jars may symbolise location and access to the dead. The jars may reflect a transition in funerary rites. At Ballateare, hollows filled with bands of sooty earth, with large and smaller lumps of charcoal and layers of ash were found associated with fragments of cremated bone as well as fragments of pottery including jars and worked flint. The pottery may represent earthfast jars that have been disturbed when the hollows were dug but, equally, they may form part of the same ritual bonfire or pyre. Earlier ritual features are rarely disturbed where sites are used over generations but rather earlier features are generally respected. It is possible that the jars were made specifically for funerary ritual. Could the jars have been fired at the same time as the bodies they came to represent? Certainly the ethnographic record is rich in accounts of pots representing people or containing souls of the dead. The completed jar could then represent the tomb of the dead, which was subsequently carefully deposited in the ground. Tim Darvill has commented on the possible significance of white quartz stones placed around the earthfast jars at Billown, just as quartz perhaps played a symbolic role at earlier tombs. Well-marked pathways of white water-worn pebbles have been noted at Cashtal-yn-Ard, the most outstanding example of a long barrow on the island. Similarly, at the passage grave on Mull Hill, nineteenth-century excavations revealed white pebbles in chambers, associated with cremation burials.

Fowler has suggested that the dead within the Manx Neolithic had complex identities that were negotiated by relations to places, animals, objects and other people. Mortuary remains often reflect the remains of many individuals mixed together and often including animal remains. Analysis of cremation deposits in the later Neolithic also suggests that elements of funerary materials were selected and removed. Here then we may envisage the products of cremations as an integral element of material culture that, together with other objects associated with people and places, were circulated in on-going social relations. The earthfast jars could then represent important elements of *loci* within the late Neolithic landscape. Their association with cremation activity may allow us to see them as nodes within the landscape where animal and human parts and objects were temporarily stored and exchanged. Whilst most of the forty or so jars on the Island come from poorly excavated contexts, those that have been carefully recorded, such as those from Billown, seem to have been marked by landscaping and positioned in relation to other elements within the Neolithic landscape. Rather than expressing individuality, perhaps the jars acted as vehicles through which the corporate dead could be reintegrated into the gestures and relations of the living.

The consideration of the earthfast jar biography, supported by archaeological evidence, archaeometric analysis, ethnographic parallel and theoretical consideration of style and symbol, has allowed us to approach these enigmatic vessels with a possible understanding of how they were made and used in the Manx Late Neolithic.

Conclusion

Until recently, few had realised that there is a snake's head at the top of Hawkes' ladder of inference. The detailed study of the production steps, made possible by the application of archaeometric analyses, and the realisation that technological acts are fully social acts, has allowed the possibility of reaching the cognitive heights at the top of the ladder without having to climb it. Technology is the root to cultural action and a key to understanding the colourful components of culture.

From the analysis of how things were manufactured, we gain access to aspects of social organisation through to the cognitive aspects of past people. Ignoring the details of production processes and viewing artefacts simply as the inevitable consequence of physicochemical determinants divorced from human agency leads to cold, dark and uninviting pasts.

5

SEARCHING FOR PROVENANCE

Introduction

There is a preponderance of studies within archaeological science that aim to determine the provenance of artefacts. Trying to identify where raw materials used for artefacts originate is a key consideration in trade and exchange studies. Whilst provenance is still a major concern amongst archaeometrists, it is not so popular in mainstream archaeology as twenty years ago. In this chapter we ask why analytical studies have concentrated on provenance, examine some of the problems associated with such studies and finally comment on their potential contribution to wider archaeological studies. New archaeologists established provenance studies to help reconstruct exchange systems since the economic sub-system held a central position in the processual understanding of social change and development. Archaeologists no longer focus on economic factors at the expense of others, such as ritual or technological, but there is still good reason to try and work out where artefacts came from. Modern provenance studies do not always interpret results solely in terms of exchange economics but now focus on ideas of ethnicity, access to resources and divergent means of expressing power.

History of provenance

Traditional approaches

Before analytical studies, art history and typological studies attempted to attribute artefacts to production centres. Such methods employ visual description of style. Individuals learnt to recognise style and attributed artefacts to production areas. Some art historians of sculpture and pottery even claim to recognise the hands of individual artists, so phrases like 'the work of the Berlin painter' become commonplace. Critics point out that such scholarship reduces itself to connoisseurship, closed to academic scrutiny. Only those who endorse the technique can recognise difference or subtleties in style. If it is possible for individuals to recognise barely perceptible differences, allowing them to attribute artefacts to individual craftspeople, it still does not prove where the artefact was produced or where the raw material came from. This has led to all sorts of arguments about itinerant craftspeople and schools of artisans working in similar styles. What is needed is a rigorous method to ascertain the source of raw material and to locate production in time and space.

Analytical approaches

Modern analytical methods offer an objective means for describing artefacts. Attribution by art-historical method must be accepted in good faith, unless all can share the eye of a connoisseur, analytical data is more open to democratic debate. Not everyone can debate tables of chemical analyses but, once fluent in the language of science, debates can ensue. Some see traditional connoisseurship and scientific analysis as exclusive as each other. We would argue that learning to converse scientifically is a much more open affair than being indoctrinated into the mystical art of art-historical connoisseurship. Scientific analyses can and *should* be much more discussible than the proclamations of art historians.

There are three basic analytical approaches to provenance studies and each may rely on variety of techniques. They are: *trace element chemical analysis, isotopic analysis* and *microstructural characterisation*.

Virtually all materials contain very low levels of 'trace' elements. Element type and concentration depends on many factors including geological formation, geographic location, technology and diagenesis. Measuring trace elements allows different sources to be given a specific trace element fingerprint. On one level, provenance studies are simple: analyse artefacts from an excavation and compare them to potential sources for a match (**51**).

Isotopic analysis relies on variations in a materials isotopic composition (**52**). Isotopes are elements with the same number of electrons and protons, hence the same chemical appearance and behaviour, but with differing numbers of neutrons, i.e. they can be a little heavier or lighter. When we determine isotopic composition we look at a single element, e.g. lead, and measure the differing weights of all the lead atoms thus characterising a material based upon its isotope 'signature'. Measuring isotopic signatures has proven to be a powerful means by which to characterise differences in similar materials. For instance, copper produced during the Bronze Age seems to have a different lead isotope signature depending on whether it was made in Cyprus, Greece, or Sardinia. This difference occurs because the different copper deposits were

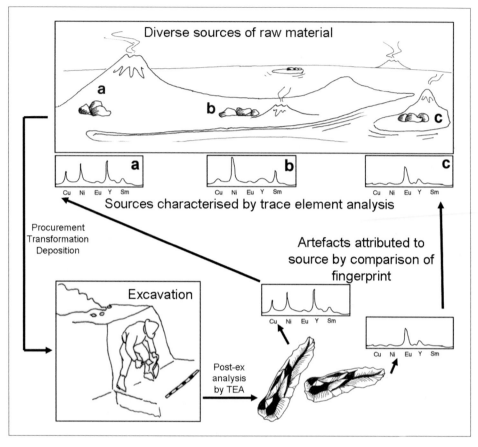

51 *The principles of provenancing by trace element analysis*

formed at different times, the older a copper deposit the more radiogenic lead isotopes present. This is great news for archaeologists looking at the exchange of copper in this period as, whilst the trace elements might all be similar, the lead isotope signature may be quite different. Although techniques such as this were initially greeted with much enthusiasm, time has shown that there are factors that complicate the application of this technique. One way around these difficulties has been to employ a combined approach that looks at trace elements and isotope signatures together.

Microstructural characterisation is an instrumentally simple means of analysis but one that requires a high degree of user skill. In contrast to the numerical compositional data of other techniques, microstructural analysis tends to be qualitative producing descriptive data. Microstructural characterisation is normally undertaken using microscopes with either polished samples or thin-sections (**53**). Occasionally, the scanning electron microscope may be used in conjunction with probe analyses (SEM-EDS). This is a favoured technique for

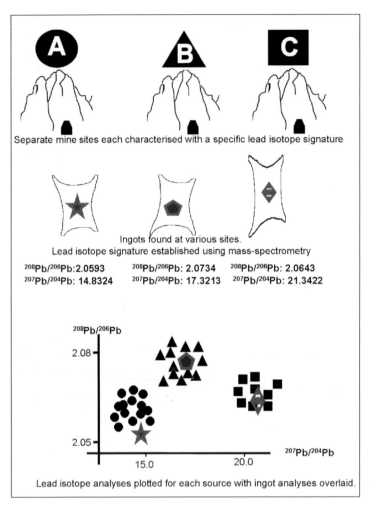

Separate mine sites each characterised with a specific lead isotope signature

Ingots found at various sites.
Lead isotope signature established using mass-spectrometry

$^{208}Pb/^{206}Pb$:2.0593 $\quad$ $^{208}Pb/^{206}Pb$: 2.0734 $\quad$ $^{208}Pb/^{206}Pb$: 2.0643
$^{207}Pb/^{204}Pb$: 14.8324 $\quad$ $^{207}Pb/^{204}Pb$: 17.3213 $\quad$ $^{207}Pb/^{204}Pb$: 21.3422

Lead isotope analyses plotted for each source with ingot analyses overlaid.

52 *The principles of provenancing by lead isotope analysis*

ceramics and lithics. By identifying the nature of the included mineral fragments and their relative proportions, a ceramic petrographer can gain a good idea of the geological environment that clay is derived from, in addition they can also get an idea of the fabric variation in a single pot type or indeed the differences among different types. This information can prove invaluable in determining provenance. Ideally, if archaeologists have excavated evidence for production, then wasters – that is failed pots discarded at the kiln site – can be compared with pots from other sites to see how similar they are and tie artefacts to production sites. Reflected light petrography is ideal for examining opaque minerals such as those encountered in metal bearing minerals, slags and, metals. Rather than noting the effect that a sample has on transmitted polarised light, reflected light petrography analyses crystal texture and the association between different minerals (**54**).

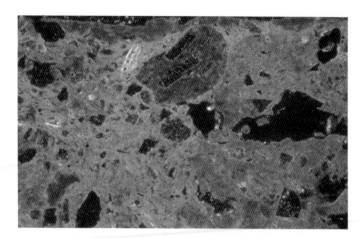

53 *Photomicrograph of ceramic thin section showing clay matrix and inclusions*

54 *Photomicrograph of a slag polished section. Central structure is Wustite (FeO)*

Early studies

Early provenance studies used trace element analysis (TEA) and micro-structural characterisation, since isotope studies are a relatively recent introduction. Early attempts successfully provenanced Aegean obsidian by TEA. Colin Renfrew and colleagues reconstructed exchange networks in the Early Bronze Age by attributing various obsidian artefacts to their source (**55**). Such studies were pivotal for our understanding of early state formation.

Obsidian is an ideal material to provenance. It is chemically homogenous, occurs in discrete locations and, in geological terms, is deposited quickly. Most importantly the chemistry of obsidian does not change in its transformation from raw material to finished artefact. The success of early provenance studies raised hopes but led to some less successful studies. Perhaps the most startling example is the so-called Stuttgart analyses (SAM) undertaken by the 'Wuttenbergisches Landesmuseum'. The aim of the SAM project was to

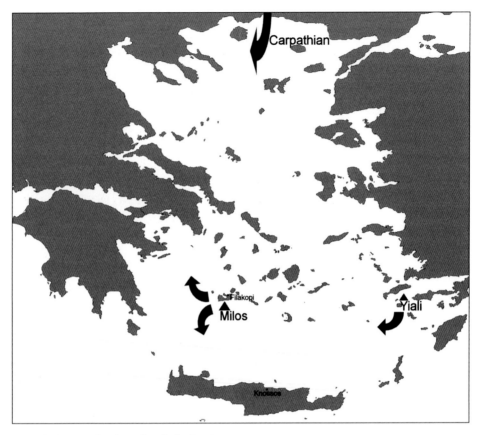

55 *The location of Melos and Yiali obsidian deposits*

analyse the trace elements of many bronze artefacts with a view of reconstructing the circulation of metal in Bronze Age Europe. Although this was a
laudable aim, some awful assumptions were made. The scale of the study was
extraordinary; most studies today work at a local or regional level because local
stylistic and chronological variation can be considered. Conversely, the
Stuttgart team aimed to address questions at a pan-European scale. Some
scholars have argued that attempts to understand data at such a wide-ranging
scale is an attempt to dominate the area of study, gaining status by asking big
questions relating to larger geographic regions and timescales. The SAM
project drilled holes in over 20,000 artefacts from all over Europe. Virtually
every national museum has a collection of bronze artefacts that has a series of
holes left by the Stuttgart team. The artefacts were then classified according to
their chemical compositions, specifically As, Sb, Ag, Ni and Bi and an attempt
was made to understand their temporal and spatial distribution.

The results of these analyses remain inconclusive and many scholars hold
that metal artefacts cannot be provenanced by their chemical composition. If

we stop to think, it soon becomes clear why the SAM analyses failed. Firstly, the elements (As, Sb, Ag, Ni and Bi) do not necessarily just reflect ore types. The SAM group had assumed that these elements reflect different types of ore and hence origin, but it was soon realised that some of them, especially arsenic, might in fact reflect the alloying of metal or some other process such as re-melting. One other problem not considered by the SAM group was that their sample came from the whole of Europe and probably sampled material from several different technological traditions. For instance, we now understand that Bronze Age inhabitants of the Alps smelted copper in a totally different way to those of the Aegean islands. Different smelting procedures could dramatically affect the way that these elements made their way through to the final copper. The SAM group was guilty of not considering the archaeological context of production and how this impacted on final artefact composition. Finally, no consideration was given to recycling and mixing of metal from different sources. A lot of time and money was spent, many artefacts partially destroyed with nothing much useful coming out of the endeavour. The widely felt failure of the SAM project has tainted science-based projects ever since. Sadly, there seems to be a reticence among archaeometrists to learn from the mistakes made in the SAM misadventure. This lesson is quite a simple one and good news for archaeologists. Prior to expensive, detailed scientific analyses, it is imperative to conduct extensive archaeological study. Had the SAM analyses been preceded by detailed investigations of copper smelting production sites it would have been realised that smelting technology was not a uniform process. Despite this many projects have been instigated recently, i.e. the Pb isotope analyses of ox-hide ingots, which ignored detailed fieldwork in favour of extensive laboratory based analysis. Scientists are too hastily diving into artefact analyses in an attempt to reconstruct whole systems of how those artefacts were exchanged whilst the archaeologists have not even started digging in order to try and understand how they were produced.

Transformative and non-transformative materials

Provenance has been undertaken on a wide variety of materials including copper alloys, flint, obsidian, glass, amber, gold, ceramics and minerals. Scientists are prepared to try to provenance almost anything that was exchanged in antiquity and has survived. The most important issue compli-cating a provenance project is whether the material of study is the product of a transformative or non-transformative technology.

Non-transformative technologies tend to be reductive technologies such as flint-knapping or stone-working; in these cases the final artefact resembles the raw material in terms of its microstructure and chemical composition. Transformative technologies, on the other hand, harbour problems since they invariably produce composite materials that cannot be easily traced back to a single source or have the signature of the predominant material obscured. Transformative technologies are fire-using technologies that modify the composition of the raw material. Such technologies include metallurgy, pottery and glass manufacturing. This is most dramatically illustrated in the case of copper metallurgy. Smelting relies upon the extraction of metal from a copper-bearing mineral. The mined ore is crushed and metal-rich fragments are then concentrated by techniques such as hand-picking. Copper–rich fragments can then be roasted in an oxidising environment or simply smelted. During smelting the metal portion of the ore will be reduced, melt and collect in the furnace. It is during this process that certain trace elements in the ore will migrate to either the metal or the slag. Often additions are made to the furnace such as charcoal and fluxes. Moreover, the furnace lining may melt and become part of the slag. All of these additions contain trace elements that partition between the slag and the metal. The final metal may be enhanced in or depleted of certain trace elements depending on whether they have a higher affinity for the slag or the metal. This is unfortunate for provenance studies since, unless this process is thoroughly understood in terms of what materials were used and how the process was acted out, it is difficult to see how archaeometrists can interpret the results of artefact and ore analyses.

In the case of glass the problem is exacerbated. Whereas copper metallurgy relies on an ore mined from a specific location, glass is a truly composite material that results from the fusion of different materials from different locations. Glass is produced by the fusion of a silica and flux. In medieval Britain the source of silica could be crushed quartz or river sands whereas the alkali source has commonly been thought to be the ash of beech trees or ferns. Since these two vital ingredients have been derived from disparate geological areas, it becomes meaningless to provenance glass back to the source of any one raw material. Scientists investigating the source of glass artefacts have tended to talk in terms of production regions rather than locating artefacts to exact sources of raw materials.

Put simply the use of fire in technological practice has the effect of obliterating any original microstructure and if the material is brought into contact with other materials, mixing of trace elements means that it is not a simple matter of comparing an analytical result of the artefact with the source. The most successful provenance studies have always been undertaken on artefacts from non-transformative processes.

Assumptions and problems of provenance

All provenance studies rely on a set of key assumptions. Provenance studies have often assumed that recycling does not occur although archaeological investigations have frequently shown such assumptions to be wrong. To avoid problems of recycling, early provenance studies on copper alloy artefacts concentrated on the Early Bronze Age since it was assumed that, at this early phase of metal use, artefacts would not have been recycled. Scholars have since suggested that recycling was perhaps practised more during this period than any other! Provenance studies of metals and glass are particularly vulnerable to assumptions concerning recycling but so are ceramics, admittedly to a much lesser degree. The documented use of grog, crushed pottery, as a temper in ceramic production reminds us that even materials which we do not normally associate with recycling can sometime be modified by such practices.

A fundamental assumption that concerns all artefacts is the extent to which the deposits of raw materials are understood. Provenance studies usually analyse an assemblage of artefacts from a single or many sites and then analyse all the known deposits of raw materials in the region. Analysis may include chemical, isotopic or microstructural characterisation or a combined approach. The results of the artefact analyses are then compared with those of the known deposits. Where an overlap or match exists it is assumed that the artefacts are derived from those deposits.

However, such simplistic interpretation assumes that all the deposits analysed today were known in antiquity and equally all those known in antiquity are known today. Moreover, it is also assumed that the composition of the samples analysed today from the specific sources bears a direct relationship to the composition exploited in antiquity. Further, when the source materials are analysed, the geographic extent of their location often determines the conclusions of the study. For instance, it is unlikely that a provenance study of copper artefacts would analyse copper deposits 2,000km away from the find spot, yet it is acknowledged that copper objects have been transported further distances in antiquity. Quite how we define the boundary of our raw materials in our study is of fundamental importance and dictates any results or conclusions.

Such issues are often glossed over or presented as a set of assumptions that we simply must accept for the study to be held valid. Although provenance is often thought to be able to identify where things come from they are better at working out where things do not come from! The possibility always remains that there is a matching source that has not been accounted for, either because it has been overlooked, or because it was exhausted in antiquity and unidentifiable today. In light of this irritating fact more confidence can be placed in saying where something does not come from rather than where it does come from. Unfortunately, archaeologists rarely ask questions in the negative.

Tied to the last point is the issue of dating and exploitation. It might be that compositional analysis or microstructural characterisation has confirmed a good match between a source and a raw material deposit. This may be supplemented by analyses of production debris meaning that the life-cycle of the artefact can be traced from 'mine' to production site, to the site where it was deposited. How can we be sure that the mine or quarry in question was exploited at the period in question? Dating of ancient metal mines, although complex, can almost always be undertaken with some degree of certainty. For metals, extraction technology gives clues to the date of exploitation. For most of Europe, prior to the Iron Age, it seems that fire-setting and pounding with stone mauls (**56**) was favoured in preference to metal tools. Fire-setting allows dating in two ways: firstly, the mine workings are easily distinguishable by their smooth and rounded form (**57**); secondly, the act of fire-setting creates soot marks and the accumulation of large quantities of charcoal which can be carbon-dated. Despite this, complications still exist. Many mines have complex multi-metallic deposits that represent several episodes of mineral deposition. It may be that a single mine-working passed through several mineral associations that were not all exploited equally through time. The exact nature of the mineral exploited at any one time needs to be assessed in light of evidence from not just the mine but also any processing and production sites. Unfortunately, it is rare to find studies that adopt such a holistic approach.

Identifying clay deposits used in ceramic production can be exceptionally problematic since clays are notoriously motile deposits prone to re-deposition elsewhere, meaning that the original clay deposit exploited in antiquity may no longer exist. It is for this reason that most ceramic studies aim to identify either a geological region from where the ceramics originate or perhaps a production site where there is evidence for kiln structures. Only when contemporary kiln structures have been identified, associated with the pottery under study and located within a likely geological region, is it reasonable to undertake prospection for probable clay sources.

Even when these demanding conditions have been satisfied, it still remains almost impossible to attribute a pot to a specific clay body with absolute certainty. Ceramics are also the result of a transformative process meaning that the final pot is an altered form of the original clay, although we often think about temper being added to the clay we should also consider that it is equally possible to remove things from it.

Appropriate characterisation of deposits has been an important point of scrutiny in recent years that can determine the success or otherwise of provenance studies. As mentioned earlier, obsidian is ideal for provenance studies, yet flint, which is used for similar functions, is not. Flint is formed by the metamorphosis of a sedimentary silicate deposit that originates from the silica skeletons of tiny marine organisms. The deposition of flint, usually in chalk, can occur over vast areas and take millions of years. Flint therefore has a highly variable chemical composition making it difficult to characterise a single deposit. Since metal mines are often multi-episodic deposits ore taken from the surface may differ in many aspects from ore retrieved at depth. Isotope compositions may vary as may trace elements and microstructure. Coupled with this the weathering of an ore body tends to differentiate certain parts of the deposit

56 *Example of a hammerstone used for the extraction of copper minerals*

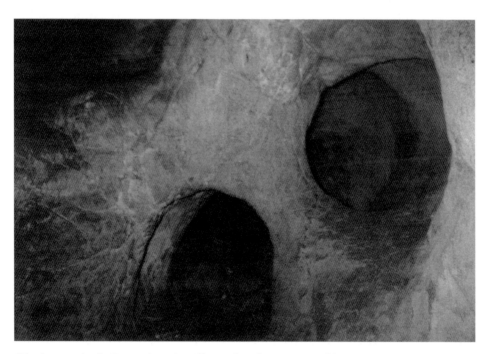

57 *An example of a Bronze-Age mine with smooth surfaces suggestive of fire-setting*

from others. It is now widely recognised that prior to sampling of an ore deposit it is essential to first undertake a detailed geological survey.

Even a well planned provenance study that acknowledges all the inherent assumptions and problems can still fail if the correct analytical method is not selected. For obsidian there is little hope of achieving a successful result using microstructural characterisation since these materials have little or no microstructure. In such cases it is necessary to rely upon trace element analysis (**58**). Ceramics containing few or no inclusions have no discernable microstructure and they too remain impossible to characterise microstructurally. It is the norm then to characterise fine wares in terms of their trace element composition. Coarseware ceramics can also be characterised by their trace element composition but it has proven to be far more useful to undertake microstructural characterisation of inclusions. The reasons for this preference become apparent when the kind of data produced is considered. Trace element data are produced in a numerical format. Having analysed our artefact or suspected raw material source, we are provided with a body of data which expresses the concentration of certain trace elements in terms of part per million (ppm) or as a percentage. Since it is usual for analyses to include a minimum of eight trace elements per sample it becomes difficult for us to compare numerical data for numerous samples with several raw material sources. It is therefore normal to use statistical procedures to gain an understanding of how similar or different artefacts are from the raw material source.

The statistical procedures normally used are forms of clustering analysis where the similarity of samples is presented in a hierarchical format. Although such procedures have proven to be effective, it is often difficult for the investigator to comprehend such complex bodies of data and an over-reliance on the statistical package can occur. Even when data sets are understood well it still comes down to the investigator to determine what constitutes a 'good' group. For instance, certain sub-groups can be lumped together to form a group or super-groups, can be split up to form distinct groups. Understanding exactly what specific concentrations of trace elements mean, especially when their geological significance is poorly understood, can be a rather abstract and numbing experience. Such problems do not arise with microstructural characterisation and this is the reason that thin section analysis of coarseware ceramics is the preferred technique. Some scholars now suggest a combined approach where trace element data are appraised in light of thin-section analysis. Unlike abstract chemical data, ceramic petrographers relate to their data directly. The data they produce are a formalised description. They follow a rigorous descriptive method and describe the colour of a ceramic matrix, the size and distribution of various mineral fragments within the sample and they identify exactly what those mineral fragments are, for instance, whether they are calcite, quartz or feldspar. The ceramic petrographer tends to have a much more intimate knowledge of the samples than an analytical chemist and,

ICP-AES

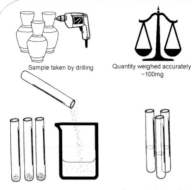

Sample taken by drilling

Quantity weighed accurately ~100mg

Sample dissolved in known volume of acid often with heating.

Prepared solutions of known sample weight in known volume.

Sampling

Most samples can be analysed by removing 100mg of material. Most ICP's require samples in the form of a solution although some allow slurries. Dissolving samples can be difficult and time consuming because of method development. It is for this reason ICP is geared towards high sample volume applications. Once dissolved the sample should be analysed, so as to prevent storage and precipitation problems. Unlike microscopic techniques where the sample can be archived, ICP samples are destroyed in the process of analysis.

Technique

Inductively coupled plasma - atomic emission spectrometry is widely used for trace element analysis (TEA) in for many materials including ceramics, lithics, metals and soils. The sample is introduced into an argon plasma at about 9000°C whereby the electrons are ripped from individual atoms. Upon cooling, electrons lose energy by emitting light. Measuring both the wavelength and intensity of these emissions allows the atom species and concentration to be determined. The technique is fast and can be automated for high sample throughput.

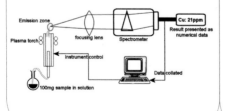

Applications

ICP-AES is the routine instrument for the determination of trace elements, but, can also be used for determining major and minor elements. It is ideally suited for metal atoms but can analyse S and P. Both provenance and technology studies make use of ICP. Its low-cost and availability make it popular in provenance studies but its precision and detection limits are inferior to NAA and ICP-MS.

Provenancing relies on being able to group artefact analyses with results from raw materials or production debris. The 'closeness' of this group depends on the inherent variation in the assemblage as well as any variation in raw material. An analysis also introduces variation which is why provenance studies require instrumentation with high precision or a low co-efficient of variation. Ideally, a technique should be used which has less variation than that naturally encountered in the material being analysed.

importantly, the data are not so abstract. Trying to understand the significance of 10ppm Sm and 13ppb Hf is a tall order but the ceramic petrographers needs only to think of the significance of the microstructural patterns they see. For instance, it the mineral inclusions are well-rounded then this tells the petrographer that the clay was probably tempered with river sands or the clay itself was derived from a once, or current, aquatic environment. If the mineral inclusions are quartz, feldspar and mica then it is obvious that the clay is not derived from a limestone area much more likely a granite-bearing area.

These are very crude examples that do not really do justice to the highly developed skills of ceramic petrographers; they do, however, illustrate the point that petrographic data allow a very real picture to be built of the environment from where clay is derived. Added to this, petrographic studies allow a better insight into the technological choices made during the manufacture of a pot and subsequent firing regimes. It is easy to determine whether a pot has been (a) wheel-thrown, (b) coil built, or (c) thumbed, by looking at the orientation of inclusions (**59**). It is ironic then that the instrumentally simplest technique can provide some of the most useful data in ceramic provenance studies. Any

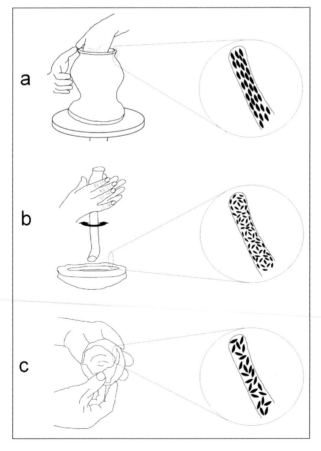

59 *How technological choice affects mineral orientation in ceramics*

provenance study of coarseware ceramics which ignores these points and chooses trace element analysis in isolation is destined not to benefit from the insights afforded by petrography but also to be the subject of mockery from more enlightened peers!

Case study: provenancing metals in the Aegean by Lead Isotope Analysis

Background

The inception of Lead Isotope Analysis (LIA) was greeted with great optimism as it was hoped to avoid many of the problems associated with trace element analysis, namely the partitioning of trace elements between slag and metal and the differential affects of unknown production. Using isotopes for provenance avoids this, since the relative concentrations of the isotopes under examination, namely Pb 204, 206, 207, 208, all behave the same during smelting. This is because they are all lead with the associated chemical characteristics of lead and the difference in their atomic weight is negligible. In reality, there may be a little bit of difference in their behaviour but at present the machines used by archaeometrists can not detect this! Put another way, the variation among ore deposits is, in most cases, greater than any variation brought about during smelting, melting and re-melting.

Initial work concentrated on archaic silver and lead deposits in the Aegean. The results were well received but the wider archaeological community engaged in research in the Archaic period was not particularly *au fait* with scientific approaches to archaeological problems. The scientific community received the results with considerable warmth and interest, whilst Archaic archaeologists felt more at home with conventional art-historical approaches to the past, the type of connoisseurship mentioned earlier. At this time Bronze Age archaeology had begun to rely more and more on scientific analyses as a way of digging deeper into certain aspects of the past, obsidian provenance had already proved successful. Foremost, amongst these scientifically conversant archaeologists was Colin Renfrew who had already published much on the origin of metallurgy in the Balkans and Northern Greece besides having effectively written the Early Bronze Age archaeology of the Cyclades; exactly the location in the Aegean where the richest sources of lead and silver were located. Renfrew suggested that the investigation extended its focus to the Bronze Age and specifically the earliest lead and silver objects associated with the Cycladic Early Bronze Age.

The contribution of LIA to this period of prehistory was significant. For the first time real scientific evidence was produced to argue which mineral deposits were exploited in the earliest phase of the Bronze Age. This was important work since it did not rely on mere speculations of archaeologists whose impressions had been formed by the painstaking study of stylistic similarities of metal artefacts and pottery assemblages. Rather, this data constituted direct conclusive evidence of exploitation zones. In terms of trying to understand the extent or scale of the interactions between regions and communities for this early phase of prehistory this was very exciting stuff.

With improvements in instrumental detection limits and the refinement of sample preparation it became apparent that, not only could silver and lead be subjected to LIA, but also copper alloys and minerals by virtue of them containing trace amounts of lead. This opened up exciting possibilities for work in the Mediterranean in terms of both early exploitation of copper and the large-scale exploitation associated with the Late Bronze Age. It was at this point that the numerous research teams working on these problems started to differ in terms of their methodology. In fact, much of the criticism launched at LIA has been aimed more at the method for sample procurement and data presentation than at the analyses themselves. The debate concerning the archaeological meaning and the analytical validity of LIA became extremely 'lively' during this later stage of research. The differing methods and claims made by various groups proved to alienate humanities-based archaeologists who started to lack faith in the technique. There seemed also to be a sense of competition regarding funding; by this time LIA projects were attracting large funds, often from humanities-based funding bodies. In part this can be understood since, if there was concern, misplaced or not, with results from flagship projects then it is only fair that it be subject to open debate. However, 'flashpoints' at some international conferences sparked seething retorts from different group members even to the point where scurrilous gossip was promulgated suggesting that some teams would not revise their results as they were involved in authentication studies and hence in the pockets of the auction houses. Associating academics that were supposedly engaged in the virtuous pursuit of objective knowledge with something as dark and unpleasant as the illicit art market was more than libellous, it was rude!

Whatever the details of intellectual disagreement, LIA did make a significant impact on the study of metals in the Aegean Bronze Age. It was generally agreed that as few as twenty well-selected ore samples from a deposit were enough to characterise it. As deposits were analysed in ever more detail, they seemed to exhibit a wider spread of results, to complicate matters that spread did not always seem to obey a normal distribution. Some researchers, rather than simply expanding the boundaries of the ore deposits, chose instead to discard 'outliers' so that the ore sources appeared to be well grouped. This was convenient for attributing artefacts to specific deposits since it prevented some ore regions overlapping to a great extent but some researchers felt this presented an unrealistic picture of the 'actual' data. In turn, such problems changed the way lead isotope data was interpreted. Whilst some research groups felt that LIA was useful for attributing artefacts to specific geological regions, other groups felt they could attribute specific artefacts to actual mining locations. In part these differences were driven by the research agendas that each group had set themselves, on the one hand those attributing artefacts to specific regions were more interested in documenting the history of metallurgical innovation, whilst, on the other hand, those attributing specific artefacts to specific mines were keen to understand the local dynamics of a particular social system. Although still surrounded by a degree of controversy, this latter approach is certainly of more utility to the archaeologist.

Compared to the frenzy of a decade ago LIA has diminished in terms of its application to understanding the inception and provenance of metals. In part this has been due to the lingering scepticism with which humanities-based archaeologists treat scientific data; this was not helped by the contention that seemed to surround the results. Nonetheless, such studies have contributed some positive aspects to our understanding of metal provenance in the Bronze Age Aegean. It may well be that the greatest contribution that LIA has to make to our understanding of early metals is not as much their precise provenance but more the extent to which metals circulated within particular regions and were exchanged across cultural boundaries.

Application to the Aegean Early Bronze Age

After initial interest in Early Bronze Age (EBA) silver and lead, the LIA concentrated on provenancing the more abundant copper-alloy artefacts on Crete and the Cyclades. Importantly, analyses extended to the production debris from smelting sites in addition to mines with known activity during this period (**60**).

Colin Renfrew located the emergence of social complexity in the EBA and the beginning of what he called the 'international spirit', a term that has come to be understood as characterising wide-ranging exchange of all sorts of exotic goods. Renfrew saw metal goods, especially daggers, stimulating this change through increasing exchange and competition for exotic goods.

On a basic level it is possible to recount the details of LIA simply in terms of provenance. Analyses of Early Bronze Age artefacts from Crete undertaken by the Oxford LIA team demonstrated that the metal used for their manufacture came predominantly from Kythnos and Lavrion. However, such a simplistic account masks the apparent complexity of the organisation of metallurgical production.

The only site that has unequivocal evidence for extraction is on Kythnos, where diagnostic hammer-stones were found in the vicinity of copper-workings in association with Early-Cycladic pottery. The only well-established Early Bronze Age smelting sites in the Cyclades and Crete are at Skouries, Kythnos and at Chrysokamino in Eastern Crete (**61**).

There is less evidence for metal objects in the Early Bronze phase 1 (EBI), than in the Final Neolithic although recently, with the re-dating of important

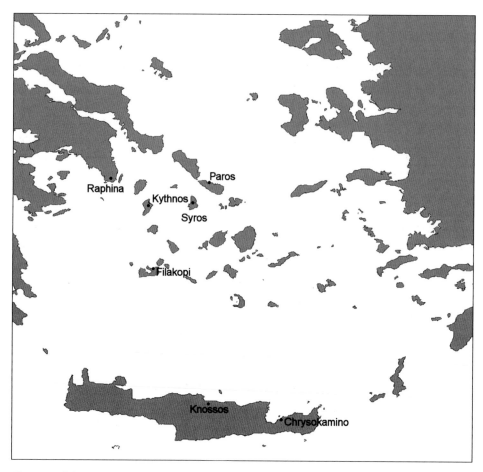

60   *Map of the Cyclades showing key sites mentioned in text*

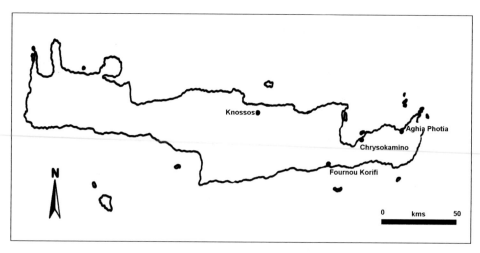

61   *Map of Crete showing location of key sites referred to in text*

burial sites such as Agia Photia in East Crete, more evidence has come to light. Virtually all the evidence of metal-work for the earliest phase of the Bronze Age comes from grave contexts and amounts to little more than daggers, small tools, wire and beads.

Apart from the sites of Kythnos and Chrysokamino mentioned above, excavations at Avyssos, Paros produced what is described as five pieces of copper slag but it is unclear what stage in the production process is represented here. There are also reported finds of early bronze copper smelting evidence from the site of Stena in Arkadia but in this case the possibility remains that it may indeed be ceramic kiln fragments! One site, Poliochni on Lemnos in the Northern Aegean, has evidence of copper slag, although again it remains unclear whether it is from casting, refining or smelting. The association of this debris with mould fragments suggests casting rather than smelting. At the site of Kastri-Chalandriani on Syros fragments of ceramic and stone mould were recovered from the EBI period. Excavations at Thermi produced metallurgical material all dating to EBI, numerous bronze artefacts, three crucibles, numerous crucible fragments and eight ceramic moulds. This appears to be melting rather than smelting evidence. Raphina in Attica produced evidence for the smelting of copper ore, including slag, a furnace bottom, bivalve moulds and tuyeres. The furnace was horse-shoe shaped with a stone lining towards one end. It appears to have produced important evidence for metallurgical practice in this period but, intriguingly, it seems very different in techno-typology to the sort of finds that are currently being reported from Chrysokamino on Crete and Skouries on Kythnos where the furnaces are some sort of inverted perforated flowerpot-shaped chimney (**62**). The evidence from Rafina is extremely intriguing and it is frustrating that the material is now lost. Since LIA has shown that the copper ores of Lavrion were used to produce artefacts that turn up on Crete, Rafina could have been the site where such ores were smelted to copper metal. Unfortunately, to date there is no convincing evidence of either Early Bronze Age mining or smelting in the vicinity of the Lavrion ore deposits.

With regards copper mineralisation on Crete, surviving evidence appears to be restricted to western and southern Crete. In the vicinity of smelting evidence at Chrysokamino there exists no known deposit of copper ore! The best-known evidence for copper mineralisation comes from Chrysostomas on the edge of the Mesara plain in southern-central Crete, where evidence of azurite and malachite was found. In west Crete, Sklavopoulou exhibits near surface evidence for copper mineralisation associated with some open-cast mining. There is no dating evidence for the exploitation of these sources but they must be considered as potential Early Bronze Age sources. More evidence comes from nearby Fournou-Korifi. Here copper-bearing pebbles were reported adjacent to the EMII settlement. The mineralisation was identified as azurite containing a respectable 2 per cent copper. Associated with this was intriguing but inconclusive evidence for copper smelting. Burnt stones and a sherd scatter approximately 15m from the settlement site and located near a water source offers the tantalising possibility of copper smelting.

The evidence for copper smelting at Skouries on Kythnos and Chrysokamino on Crete is remarkably similar. Lead isotope analysis has produced a remarkable picture of how mining and metallurgy were organised. Firstly, it was noted that, although there is good evidence for mining on Kythnos in the vicinity of Skouries, the lead isotope signature of copper prills included in the slag does not match that of the ore sampled from the copper mine. Minerals from other deposits in the Cyclades, namely Seriphos, were brought to Kythnos where they were smelted with ores from Kythnos! Equally remarkable are the results that suggest Kythnian ores were smelted at Chrysokamino. Thus artefacts with a Kythnian isotope signature may well have been derived from ores mined on Kythnos but were turned into copper in Crete! Quite where this leaves us in terms of thinking about provenance is uncertain; an artefact with a Kythnian isotope signature may come from Crete or Kythnos! To summarise the contribution of LIA in the study of metallurgy in the Aegean Early Bronze Age, most of the Minoan artefacts on Crete are derived from ores which come from Lavrion, the Cycladic Islands and, perhaps, a little from Cretan deposits. However, smelting evidence at Kythnos suggests that more than just Kythnian ores were smelted.

The presentation of data from provenance studies is problematic. Relations are established between geographical areas on the basis of comparing the analytical representations of the material evidence that is recovered archaeo-logically. This distribution 'pattern' is itself seen to represent the process of exchange, a process that is rarely elucidated in provenance studies. Archaeologists rarely account for how these distributions come about. There is a reticence to critique the data and consider how specific social practices create artefact distributions. One thing is certain regarding metallurgy in the Early Bronze Age: copper neither smelted itself nor moved itself between islands. Skilled individuals performed acts of production and there seems no compelling reasons why we should not consider the people smelting at Chrysokamino as the same people who were mining on Kythnos. The same individuals may also have transported ores and metals between islands and ulti-mately passed finished artefacts on to others.

Populating the results of LIA with active individuals allows us to envisage how they might have been affected by being involved in such acts. It seems accepted that access to prestige goods was important in constructing an indi-vidual identity in the Aegean Early Bronze Age. A sense of exoticness may not necessarily be limited to the artefacts themselves. Those involved in their production and transport would have appeared as dextrous, cosmopolitan indi-viduals who may have themselves recanted exotic tales from far-off places to the local inhabitants of Crete. It would be these same individuals who were capable of bestowing status on others by entering into exchange with metal

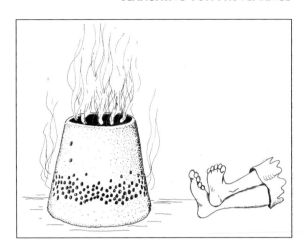

62 *Hypothetical reconstruction of an EBA Aegean copper-smelting furnace*

artefacts. Since many metal goods in EBI are found in a burial context, metal may have been considered to some degree sacred. Marcel Mauss has pointed out how those with access to the sacred have an almost inexhaustible source of power. Seen in this light LIA data can contribute much more than simply understanding where artefacts came from. Understanding the wide-ranging spatial movements of those involved in metallurgy may well have provided knowledge and resources with which to institutionalise personal power into enduring social practices.

Application to the Late Bronze Age Mediterranean

Excavation of shipwreck sites such as the Ulu Burun and Kas wrecks have shown, in stunning detail, the quantities and range of exotic materials that were in circulation during the Late Bronze Age (LBA). The inventory of finds for the Ulu Burun wreck reads like a shopping list for a Knightsbridge department store. What form do such extensive trade networks take? The one thing that archaeologists can be sure of is that artefacts and resources do not move by their own accord. The Ulu Burun shipwreck suggests that at least some exchange was well organised perhaps even under palatial control.

Amongst the stunning finds from the Ulu Burun wreck were an extraordinary quantity of copper ingots that supported the idea that copper was being transported in significant quantities during the Late Bronze Age. These ingots were a very specific type known as ox-hide ingots, because of their shape. They have been found over much of the Mediterranean and are even depicted in Egyptian Tomb paintings (**63**). An understanding of which regions were participating in the production of copper is important for reconstructing exchange networks. If it were possible to reconstruct the exchange networks then it would be a very interesting question to ask exactly how production was organised in these areas and what, if any, was the benefit of engaging in exchange.

Early in the study of copper ox-hide ingots, they were thought to represent the primary product of smelting. This was an important point since primary smelting products were unlikely to be the product of recycling or re-melting (see above). Experiments undertaken by John Merkel found that these assumptions were not safe. Merkel undertook a campaign of experimental archaeology reconstructing a copper-smelting furnace based on evidence from Timna. Merkel found that, during primary smelting, copper did not form at the base of a furnace in a reservoir to be poured into an ox-hide ingot mould. Instead Merkel found that copper settled in the bottom of the furnace as small discrete conglomerates often mixed with some slag. These needed to be re-melted in a furnace and then finally cast into an ox-hide ingot. This evidence suggested smelting and ingot casting might be spatially dislocated. Were the copper scraps transported elsewhere for re-melting where they could possibly be mixed with metal from other sources and even scrap? This was important for lead isotope studies and was supported when chemical analyses of ingots from Ras Sharma were found to contain levels of tin which, presumably, must have come from recycling tin bronze scrap.

Reconstruction of exchange networks could only be addressed once Mediterranean copper deposits were characterised. This was considered possible with twenty suitably-located samples. Although this seems sensible, some mineral deposits had highly variable lead isotope signatures. This was especially true when a mine had several episodes of mineralisation which reinforces the need for a thorough geological understanding before simply picking ores randomly. An extensive number of sites were analysed by the LIA teams with mineral deposits characterised at Lavrion, the Cyclades, Cyprus, Egypt, Jordan, Sardinia, Bulgaria and Spain.

This wide-ranging approach was in part stimulated by the way the Bronze Age had been conceptualised, a period of far-reaching political relationships underpinned by the exchange of exotic goods. In light of this, it was suspected that LIA would show material moving in large quantities around the Mediterranean. Although it is certainly true that ox-hide ingots were moving around the Mediterranean this was the exception rather than the norm. The Oxford LIA team have argued cogently that most regions catered for their own copper supply with 70 per cent of copper in a region being home-produced. However, approximately 30 per cent of copper represents imports. For the Aegean, Cyprus is the main source of this imported copper with Lavrion acting as the regional production centre.

When first discussed in the academic community, this caused uproar. Perhaps the most surprising case was Sardinia where many of the ox-hide ingots discovered were from Cyprus. What was so shocking was that Sardinia was rich in copper ores, so why would they be importing copper from Cyprus? Rather than accepting this result and trying to understand what it might mean, many archaeologists rejected LIA as a useful provenancing tool. This was surprising since

63 *Detail from an Egyptian tomb painting showing oxhide ingots being carried*

Cypriot artefacts had already been identified from Sardinian excavations. The rejection of the Sardinian results was more to do with how they confounded the minds of archaeologists and other scientists than the result itself. Some archaeologists have very sensibly suggested that copper, no matter where it was from, has an inherent value, as it is an ideal commodity that can be converted into artefacts. Cypriot ingots in Sardinia need not then to be considered so peculiar. If the oxhide ingot represents a recognisable form of copper it can act as a unit of exchange for other commodities either in Sardinia or elsewhere.

Despite the work of the LIA projects, virtually nothing is known about how production was organised and the range of technologies employed. Only recently have inroads been made into the archaeology of production in Cyprus with the stunning finds and excavations undertaken by Lina Kassianidou. There still remains a desperate need to investigate the context and control of production and to examine how exchange was organised.

LIA has been presented as a technique that can establish where copper ingots originated. However, some scholars have suggested that the LIA signature could be used in a more meaningful way avoiding the problematic assumptions associated with provenance. LIA could be used to explore the relatedness of metal-work assemblages and to comment on the degree of recycling being practised in a specific phase. Tightly clustering groups could suggest the metal in circulation had become homogenised through repeated recycling, whilst loosely clustered groups suggest metal was deposited without recycling or that many ore sources were exploited (**64**). Such novel applications may well rekindle interest in LIA.

Conclusions

Provenance studies, although currently unpopular, remain an important element of archaeological endeavour. They should not simply be seen as a way

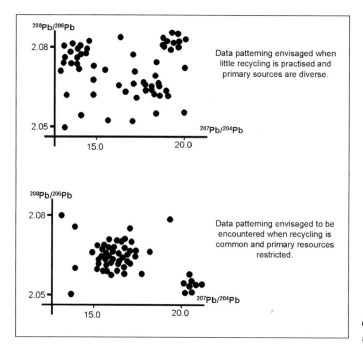

64 *Using LIA to understand metal recycling*

of reconstructing exchange mechanisms but more as a way of understanding aspects of choice, action and extending understandings of agency beyond the immediate locale of the 'site'. Many of the problems associated with provenance relate to the fossilised methodologies employed by archaeometrists. Again, there is a need for scientists to be involved in fieldwork and in direct liaison with field archaeologists at the beginning of projects.

Careful consideration of methodology is the key to a successful provenance study. In the Early Bronze Age, Aegean LIA provides such a useful set of data because it concentrates on a specific time period and focuses on a well-defined region. A key methodological point is to focus analysis on production evidence that is thought to be contemporary with mining sites. This is an exceptional situation. This can be considered to constitute a recommendation for such studies to be aimed at regional tightly focused projects where the archaeology of production, especially its scale and organisation, are established prior to the commencement of provenance studies. Scientists should be restricted from jumping hastily into lab-based artefact studies in an attempt to reconstruct exchange mechanisms until the context of production and consumption is understood archaeologically.

It remains to emphasise the point that provenance studies are exactly that, they tell us about provenance, that is, where things come from. Archaeologists on the other hand are, or at least should be, more interested in asking how they got where they were and what this meant to those involved in the production, distribution and consumption of these materials.

6

EXPLORING CHANGE

Introduction

Archaeology explores changes in long-term processes and in aspects of how past peoples chose to live their lives. From the settlement, economic and subsistence patterns of human geography, two indicators of developments in society, it is possible to piece together important stories involving change. Traditionally, 'the past' has been structured in terms of characteristic material culture patterns. Scandinavian archaeologist Christian Thomsen first attempted this in the nineteenth century when he developed the now ubiquitous 'three age system' of stone, bronze and iron. Variations on this major materials-based theme have been introduced such as the 'Chalcolithic', 'Eneolithic', or copper age that precedes the Bronze Age in parts of Europe.

The materials-based approach to subdividing prehistory neatly avoids the complexities of human agency. The explanatory engine driving our under-standing of 'the past' is on auto-cruise and fuelled with science in the form of social and technological evolution. We can very easily, almost naturally, fall into the trap of thinking that the past actually happened in neat chronological order and forget that it is, in reality, a product of now. As a result archaeologists describe, categorise and label material remains, but rarely fully explain them. This chapter explores the interplay of scientific dating techniques and their relationship to the interpretation of archaeological deposits. An approach that views the notion of agency as important, needs to acknowledge time as an important component in the field of analysis. Determining the time of action is fundamental to ordering evidence into a temporal framework that is essential for interpretations of change.

Concepts of time and dating

Physically, we experience the passing of time through the movements of the heavenly bodies and the passing of the seasons. Biologically, we experience time through growth and the aging process. Metaphysically, we include time as a central concept integral to others such as being, knowing, identity and space. The biological, physical and metaphysical experience of passing time for human beings has become so culturally enmeshed with other aspects of our lives that we have effectively 'domesticated' time. Moreover, a particular perspective on time that relates to the scientific West has come to dominate our present day understanding of time. This understanding is linear. Having been raised on 'news bulletins', countdowns to rocket launches and millennial events, we tend to subconsciously embrace time as an orderly, linear, procession of events and their consequences. We unquestioningly accept that time has been captured, defined and measured by scientists. One second is precisely defined as the duration of 9,192,631,770 periods of radiation corresponding to the transition between two hyperfine levels of the ground state of caesium 133. Atomic clocks are used to precisely determine calendars, timetables, deadlines, international trading, navigation, air traffic control and, as such, permeate many aspects of our lives.

For most of us it is hard to conceptualise time beyond tales from our parents, home movies, fading photographs and diary accounts of earlier generations. It becomes increasingly difficult to conceptualise the time–depths involved in the archaeological practice of imagining the lives of people beyond historical record. This is most clearly illustrated by the persistence of the short chronology based on the bible that was developed in the seventeenth century by Archbishop Ussher who established the beginning of the human story and the creation of the world at 4004BC. He did this by adding up the generations of family connections from the bible. Human generations are measured in periods of roughly thirty years, generally reckoned as the average time in which children are ready to take the place of their parents. The generational measure of time might be easier to conceptualise. There have been about sixty-seven generations since the birth of Christ, or seventeen generations since Columbus 'discovered' America, or 176 generations between us and the oldest naturally mummified human remains, the so called Iceman of the Tyrolean Alps.

Even so it becomes difficult to conceptualise generational time when we begin looking at the earliest evidence for modern humans in Europe. For example, radiocarbon dating of cave paintings in Europe from Chauvet Cave, France have measured their age to be about 1,067 generations old. Modern humans that were physically identical to us emerged some 5,000 generations ago probably in Africa. In Africa the human story stretches back further still with evidence of hominid forms that were leading towards the genus *Homo*. Fossil remains of Australopithecines, the most famous of which in the popular imagination has to be Lucy, are separated from us by 106,666 generations. Archbishop Ussher's short chronology takes us back only 200 generations, just 4 per cent of the estimated chronology for anatomically modern humans, and only 0.2 per cent of Lucy's timeline. Little wonder then that the realisation of the great antiquity of people beyond the biblical framework was slowly won from years of ridicule for anyone daring to suggest anything other than the short chronology, the time-depths involved are literally unimaginable with respect to our personal time-frames.

For humans the cultural expression of time, of the past, present and the future are wonderfully diverse. Some societies visualise time as a spiral, with past present and future twisting in on itself and crossing over. Ancestral time can be mingled with that of the present at certain places in special ceremonies. For other groups, the past exists alongside the present in parallel, but located geographically in taboo zones. Some cultures, relative to the views of others, are travelling backwards in time towards a dreamtime. Others may be heading for predicted disasters. Some people in Western society head towards a religious apocalypse that will result in the end of aging and time standing still, for eternal happiness for the good and eternal nothingness and death for the wicked. For those that are not touched by religion and prefer the 'scientific' approach, we head towards a physical apocalypse in the form of the end of our solar system, when the finite fuel core of the sun finally runs out. The brief exploration of generational time as an attempt at comprehending time-depth, our attempts at unravelling modern definitions of time and the physical, biological and metaphysical experience of passing time should allow us the realisation that far from being a reassuringly solid concept, we all relate to time in different ways. It is only since 1884 that the world has had an international standard of time, now formally known as Universal Time, and dominated by an objective, scientific approach to recording and expressing time.

Some people lead such interesting, full and rewarding lives that they are said to live several lifetimes. The oldest authenticated human, Jeanne Louise Calment, lived in France through the shrinking world of communications. She was born in 1875 shortly before the telephone was patented and nine years before the international standard of reckoning time was defined. The only means of travelling across the Atlantic when she was a young woman was by boat, a journey that took over four days by ocean liners such as the *Titanic*. Jeanne was thirty-seven years old when the *Titanic* sank. By 1937, when she was sixty-two and the *Hindenburg* zeppelin disaster put an end to transatlantic airship travel, a crossing could be made in just two days. The Second World War saw the development of jet engines that revolutionised air travel. By Jeanne's 101st birthday, commercial flights to America had begun in Concorde that cut the journey time to just three and a half hours. By 1995 and the passing of Jeanne's 120th birthday the telephone had been usurped by the world wide web and e-mails as the most common form of transatlantic contact. Jeanne died two years later in 1997, only a few years away from her time-frame having overlapped three centuries and two millennia.

Jeanne may have witnessed amazing cultural transformations, but even her relatively long personal time-frame was not significant enough to allow her to witness much in the way of geological transformations. What of geological time? This is the time taken for rocks to form, for coastlines to be eroded, for whole continental plates to move against each other. It is within these vistas of geological time that human time-frames become meaningless, even within the expanded concept of generational time. Geologists discuss time-frames where the margins of error in measuring them within our own time-frames are vast. It is difficult to see these imperceptibly slow processes as dynamic, but if we were able to fast-forward geological time we would see continents moving, mountains rising or eroding away and ice sheets waxing and waning.

Consideration of geological and generational time-frames, together with discussions of our scientific and other culturally conditioned definitions of time allow us to play with time. What if for example, time could be considered as a physical phenomenon, as it is inextricably part of other physical phenomena such as sound waves? Now consider the famous philosophical and physical conundrum concerning the tree in the forest where there are no higher organisms around. If the tree were to be struck by lightening, on falling, would it make a noise? It would generate sound waves, but if there are no biological entities capable of hearing the collapse, then surely there is no such thing as 'noise' involved in this scenario. Similarly time, as a physical phenomenon, does not exist, unless there are living creatures around to experience the passing of time. Since everything in the past is now dead, there are no entities to experience the past, the past therefore does not exist, there is only now as experienced by *you*. Just as the future does not exist, only in our imaginations, so too the past is created in the present from the evidence that suggests to us that generations of people before us have experienced their own presents. But, hold on . . . now is always over by the time we consider it. Maybe the only experiential reality in time is the anticipation of the immediate future. Time as we experience it, is simply the interface between the past and the future and the swirling currents of memory, perception and anticipation that accompanies the time-front. For some such a playful attitude to the past is unacceptable as it flies in the face of robust scientific enquiry. It also erodes the sense of safety and familiarity that surrounds us in the form of our own cultural attitudes towards concepts of time and institutions that rely on other concepts such as heritage and tradition. For even the most celebrated of physicists, the definition and nature of time was illusory. Albert Einstein wrote in a letter four weeks before his death: 'People like us who believe in physics know that the distinction between the past, present and future is only a stubbornly persistent illusion'.

Concepts of dating and 'changing'

The scientific dating techniques that are used in archaeological practice represent a fascinating area in the relationship of science to understanding the lives of past people and how we are related to them through the passage of time. Bringing the material remains, the action, choice, place and historical contingency together at a point in time is the stuff of archaeological interpretation that involves 'dating' and chronology building.

The motor of archaeological explanation is change, without it archaeology becomes mere description of snapshots somewhere in time. Understanding change allows us to put the snapshots together to create a moving picture. We can imagine a particular subject of interest, for example a series of excavations and collections of data from them and their analysis as a series of imaginations or images. Cutting them together into a workable sequence to animate them into a satisfying movie with good continuity and a decent story line involves dating or chronology building.

The ability to place an event, 'culture', or process into a time-frame, gives us an opportunity to explore ideas about change. The predominant model, until relatively recently has been to presume directional change towards complexity and progress. This model has been hard-wired into Western thinking about concepts of social and technological progress. Aspects of rethinking the past rooted in post-modern approaches involve deconstruction and critical theory. Together with advances in scientific dating techniques and archaeological evidence, the theoretical catalysts of deconstruction and critical theory have enabled new approaches to exploring change.

The persistent old chronological order that was so strongly linked to materials and ideas of social complexity has now been reduced to little more than arbitrary terms. There were metals in the Neolithic and shades of animal husbandry and domestication of plants in the Mesolithic. There is no longer a comfortable tessellation of technological and social progress. It seems the people who lived before us have the ability to surprise us and challenge our need to see ourselves as the inevitable consequences of evolutionary changes.

Changes in dating: the historical backdrop

The emergent discipline of archaeology was comfortable in relating artefacts to historical frameworks that associated objects through their typical characteristics with more distant artefacts that could be tied to datable objects through historical records, such as Egyptian Ruler lists. The historical documents fitted in nicely with Ussher's short chronology. One of the effects of Wallace and Darwin's theory of evolution had been to galvanise the notion of the emerging Victorian Empire as the pinnacle of a whole series of progressive enterprises that were seen to be natural and scientifically provable. The use of scientific explanation to promote theories such as biological and social evolution was especially potent. Leading scientists of the day fed politicians with factoids and hypotheses that permanently coloured colonial policy. For example it was not until the 1960s that policy towards resettlement of aboriginal babies with white families, to give them a 'better' life, was ended. Aboriginals had been seen as a cul-de-sac of social evolution, living fossils doomed to a harsh desert life, rather than supremely well-adapted and innovative cultures. Clearing them in some places for the inevitable progress of colonial settlement, often by shooting them, was seen by some to be the kindest way forward in the 1880s.

The development of scientific dating techniques in the twentieth century has enabled the realisation that the antiquity of people was far deeper back in time than could possibly be imagined by a society raised with Ussher's timeframe. The development of potassium-argon dating in particular has been essential in the subsequent unfolding of the major sequences of fossil evidence of Australopithecine chronology in Africa and the development of our own genus, *Homo*. Potassium-argon dating focused on the geochemical dating of layers of rock many hundreds of thousands, even millions of years old. To many archaeologists, the far-off story of human evolution seemed remote and irrelevant to their research interests. In the main, the comfortable historically based chronologies of Europe that relied on models of inspiration and diffusion of innovations such as farming and metallurgy, held firm.

Radiocarbon dating was largely embraced and welcomed in the New World, whilst treated with some hostility in the Old World. Radiocarbon was a technique that, theoretically, could help in the chronology building of key questions of the current geological epoch, the Holocene. The development of hunter-gatherer complex societies, the advent of domestication and agriculture, the spread of metallurgy and chronological details of culture group interactions all fell within the time span of the radiocarbon technique, roughly the last 45,000 years. The refinements of carbon-14 dating involving dendro-chronological, tree-ring, calibration of radiocarbon years, verified the scientific robustness of the technique. With calibration came the so-called radiocarbon revolution, a shattering realisation that European chronologies were wrong.

A chronological fault line across Europe forced a rethink of chronology building and set in motion a series of far-reaching changes to archaeological practice. As the shock waves of the radiocarbon revolution reverberated around the archaeological community, it was realised that the traditional culture-history approach, dominated as it was by descriptions and typological relationships of artefacts, was theoretically and scientifically impoverished. As prehistory was being re-written, the path was open for other new ideas and new scientific approaches to be adopted.

In the arena of scientific dating then, the conceptual gap between archaeologist and scientist is significant. The major problem is that many archaeologists see scientific dating as a powerful science that has the ability to transport us back into a scientifically verifiable past. We have already argued that such a past does not exist. Appearing as trustworthy people wearing white-coats, many accept the data returned from chronometric laboratories as dates, despite the fact that we are reminded by those handing us the data that they are not dates and must be subject to interpretation. The empirically based data that suggests to us that artefact 'a' is 'x' number of years old is subject to many questions that affect the reliability of the date with respect to our archaeological interpretation. Even if we can resolve those questions and be certain of our date, a major challenge arises as to how the date is *conceptualised* within our archaeological interpretation.

Relative and absolute dating

Just as we today deal with different scales of time, precise at the start of a race, less so for the start of a meeting and approximate at the start to a love affair, so archaeologists deal with different scales of dating, relating to different kinds of questions concerning change. There is a division of dates that can be relative or absolute. A relative date determines the temporal relationship of one object or process to another within a cultural sequence. Absolute dates determine the age of a material in relation to the present, how old is an object or deposit, or an inferred event?

Relative dates are used widely and simple principles of stratigraphy can be used to determine a relative chronology, as a general rule notwithstanding natural or cultural disruptions, something discovered deeper in the stratigraphy is older than something higher in the stratigraphy (**66**). As popularity of pottery types waxes and wanes through time, it is possible to relatively date the layers of a site depending on the amounts of different classes of pottery present. This is known as seriation or typological dating. Detailed chronologies can be established between sites through association of commonly occurring suites of artefact. In some situations the use of typological dating is more secure and offers greater accuracy than attempting to date deposits using absolute dating techniques. For example, the Dragendorf series describes the style changes of different patterns of a widespread type of high class Roman fine tableware pottery known as Samian (**65**). The dates of changing styles can be dated to within a decade or so.

Absolute dates are derived from various physicochemical properties of the samples being measured. The term 'absolute' sounds scientifically robust and safe, almost as if an absolute date is unquestionably and 'absolutely' right. However, as with all archaeological endeavours, they are open to interpretation

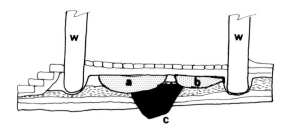

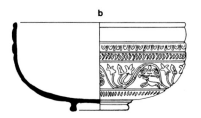

65 *Mould-made Samian bowls with raised decoration and red slipped are useful chronological markers.* Redrawn from Anderson, 1984

66 Above: *Stratigraphic relationships and relative dating.* Redrawn from Barker, 1977

and revision. Absolute dates are less commonly determined in practice than relative dates. Nevertheless, absolute dating techniques offer crucial windows into the past, especially in those situations where there are no rich associations of relative style changes that can be correlated to objects of known dates.

Understanding scientific dating techniques

The scientific advances that have been made in the field of archaeologically relevant dating techniques cannot be overstated. This area of archaeological science has been one of the most consistently successful disciplinary endeavours that have resulted in far reaching developments within archaeological practice and expectations. Figure **67** provides a summary of materials and the major dating methods that can be used to date them. Some 76 dating methods are available to geoscientists and archaeologists. Some techniques are standard (K-Ar, radiocarbon, thermoluminescence), others are routine (ESR and optical dating) and yet further techniques are in development such as beryllium-10 for marine sediments, calcium-41 for bones and calcareous sediments and calcium diffusion and cation ratios in plaster and rock art.

Technological innovations have allowed the measurement of smaller samples, extended the range of useful materials and deepened the applicable date range. Consideration of errors introduced through misunderstanding of context, issues of contamination or sample heterogeneity are as relevant with the new techniques as they are for the old. Scientific dating is not a straightforward process providing data for the obligatory appendix that automatically adds weight to a

Technique	volcanic	glass	obsidian	unburnt sediment	burnt flint stone	slag	pottery baked earth	stalag-calcite	shells	tooth enamel	bone antler ivory teeth	wood plant seeds etc.
dedrochronology												●
radiocarbon							◐	○	○	◐	●	●
potassium - argon	●											
Uranium - series	◐							●	◐	◐	◐	
Fission tracks	●	◐	◐			◐						
luminescence	◐			●	●	○	●	◐				
ESR	○				○		○	●	◐	◐	○	
amino acid									◐	◐	◐	
hydration			◐									
magnetism	◐			◐			◐	○				

67 *Table of commonly datable materials and dating techniques. Shaded circle area indicates increasing confidence. Redrawn from Aitken, 1990*

report. The validity of comparisons of results from different materials and different laboratories involves wider issues of the use of standards and the need for inter-laboratory calibration. Similarly the raw data from laboratories must undergo appropriate statistical analysis, such as calibration for radiocarbon methods, before they can be useful to archaeological interpretation.

The techniques outlined in **67** represent those that are closely associated with developments in archaeological science as well as those that are standard or routine in most literature. These techniques are divided into eight major groups.

Radiogenic noble gas techniques

Potassium-argon and uranium-helium dating measure the amount of noble gas that is produced by the predictable radioactive decay of heavy elements within parent rock. As the molten rock allows gases to escape, these techniques measure the time proportional build-up of trapped radiogenic gases following solidification. These techniques can therefore be used to date volcanic eruptions and help to determine the dates of fossils sandwiched between eruptions. The half-lives (time taken for radioactive materials to exponentially decay by half) for potassium and uranium are very long, enabling broad dating ranges for these techniques.

Radioactive equilibrium/disequilibrium techniques

There is a large selection of radioactive materials contained within rocks and sediments that have different radioactive decay chain products. By measuring the ratios of various parent elements and the products of decay, the age of the deposit can be calculated. These techniques rely on assumptions of the behaviour and nuclear chemistry of geological deposits and their formation through processes of dissolution, solution and precipitation.

Radiogenic/cosmogenic nuclides

There is a wide range of radioactive elements that are produced either by radiation bombardment in the atmosphere (cosmogenic) or as the result of long-lived decay chains (radiogenic). These elements can enter into natural cycles of geological and biological systems. Through understanding the processes of exponential decay and the nature of the distribution and behaviour of the systems in which such radiogenic and cosmogenic materials are involved, it is possible to devise measurements that will allow the dating of various events. Carbon-14 is an example of a cosmogenic nuclide that allows the determination of the age since death of organic matter.

Particle track dating techniques

Solid rocks containing unstable isotopes such as uranium–238, sustain microscopic damage as a result of the energy released during fission reactions. This infrequent form of radioactive decay involves the spontaneous fission of the isotope into two fragments that are forced apart with such force that they displace surrounding atoms in the crystal lattice to form damage pathways known as fission tracks. Other forms of decay, known as alpha recoil, also

68 *Overlapping tree-rings allow the creation of a continuous chronology*

produce damage tracks. By counting tracks that accumulate at known rates and determining the concentration of uranium in a sample, it is possible to determine the date of solidification of the rock or glass as the tracks will accumulate through time.

Radiation dosimetry techniques

In certain minerals such as quartz, ionising radiation present in surrounding deposits, results in electrons becoming trapped within the crystal lattice. Some electrons remain trapped almost indefinitely until released by heat which releases trapped electrons in the form of light. Luminosity is determined by the amount of electrons trapped, which itself depends on the dose of ionising radiation, the dose time and the susceptibility of the material to be affected by radiation. If the dose rate and sensitivity of the material are known, then the age of the sample can be calculated. Optical dating techniques are an extension of the same phenomenon but electron traps are sensitive to light, rather than heat. Whereas heat-sensitive trap gives an age of last heating event, light-sensitive traps date the burial or obscuration event.

Trapped electrons in biological material caused by ionising radiation can be quantified through electron spin resonance. This technique does not liberate electrons from their traps but rather makes them spin in different orientations. This technique is repeatable and useful for early hominid studies.

Chemical reaction techniques

Some techniques rely on the chemical reaction of materials. As rocks are exposed to weathering they develop layers whose thickness is time dependent. This can be measured to estimate the exposure time. Other techniques involve the phenomenon of water absorption (hydration) into newly exposed fracture surfaces on obsidian. There are further techniques that measure the optical qualities of amino acids that make up the organic fraction of samples such as shell and bone. In life such structures have a particular orientation but, on death, the process of decay results in a gradual re-orientation, known as racemisation. This effect is in part time dependant and, when quantified, can allow an age since death to be calculated.

A major problem with all chemical techniques is that the reactions are not only time dependent but also vary according to unknown factors such as temperature, pressure and other environmental factors that cannot be precisely determined. This contrasts with those techniques that measure isotope decay, as this process is not affected by environmental parameters. Chemical-reaction based techniques are therefore used as relative dating techniques or to verify others.

Palaeomagnetic techniques

These techniques are based on cyclical but unpredictable changes in the earth's magnetic field over time. Such change results from the nature of the molten iron core of the earth. When materials containing iron oxides are heated, the magnetic poles of these oxides align in sympathy with the earth's magnetic field, so-called thermoremanent magnetism. This alignment is frozen into the material upon cooling. By comparing the orientation with standard reference data, it is possible to calculate the date of the heating event. This technique is known as archaeomagnetic dating. A related technique, palaeomagnetic dating independently dates (usually through carbon-14) lake bed sediments that record magnetic change through time related to depth (it is through this process that local archaeomagnetic calibration curves are constructed).

Climatic techniques

Some techniques date climatically influenced phenomena through the record of annual cycles. One of the most important and only true absolute technique is dendrochronology. If counted accurately, tree-rings, indicate the precise age of the tree. Good and poor growth years mean that characteristic patterns develop that allows a series of dead trees to be cross-matched to form a continuous chronology. Comparison of timbers in preserved structures with the chronology can therefore allow precise dating (**68**). Each growth ring is composed of materials made in a given year. It is therefore possible to carbon date wood of an age that is known precisely by drilling a sample from each ring. It is through this process that calibration curves are constructed for radiocarbon dating.

The dendrochronological timescale dates back some 11,800 years and can be correlated to other climatic techniques that stretch back much further in time. One such technique is ice core chronologies. These rely on counting seasonal layers of ice and compacted snow that form continuous records in polar ice caps. Such layers can be analysed in terms of structure, air bubble content, dust layers deposited each summer and chemical analysis of seasonal variations of oxygen isotopes incorporated into the layers. A continuous ice core record has been obtained by a drilling research programme that dates back to 160,000 years.

Radiocarbon dating

The development of carbon-14 or radiocarbon dating is one of the rarities of the archaeological discipline. Developed in the 1950s with archaeology in mind as the major user group, it contrasts against most other techniques, which are borrowed from related disciplines. Today, archaeology remains a minor user group. Most commercial laboratories cater for prospection companies and other disciplines where accuracy of date, in archaeological terms, is not important.

Radiocarbon age estimates have to be calibrated to convert them into approximations of calendar dates, as one of the fundamental assumptions of the technique that radiocarbon production has remained constant through time,

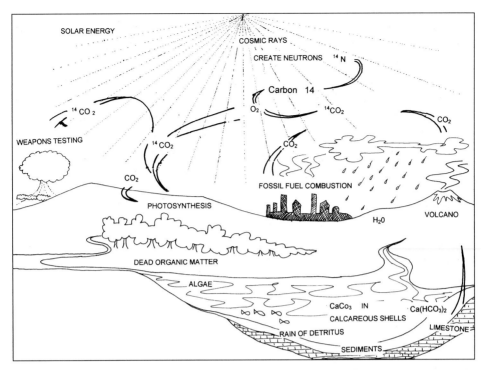

69 Above and right: *The C–14 cycle*

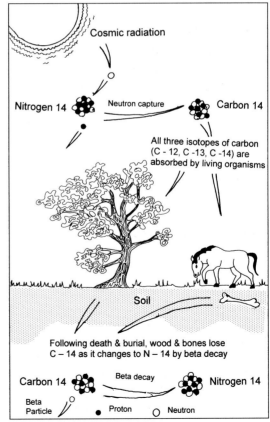

has been proven false. Different organic materials have better or worse potentials to produce accurate dates owing to their relationship with the carbon-14 cycle (**69**), and differentially incorporate contaminating materials. Knowledge of the various complexities of the technique is required in order to use radiocarbon age estimates effectively.

Radiocarbon age estimation

All life on earth depends on the energy of the sun and the combination of carbon dioxide and water through the process of photosynthesis in green plants. Through the biological processes of photosynthesis, eating and digestion and reproduction, all living matter contains carbon that has been fixed originally through photosynthesis into sugars and subsequently transformed and modified through the complexities of the food web into the organic matter that makes up all living things.

Carbon exists in three forms or isotopes, two of which, carbon-12 and carbon-13, are stable and the third, carbon-14, which is radioactive. This radioactive form of carbon is produced by cosmic radiation colliding with nitrogen in the upper atmosphere.

$$N_7^{14} + \text{cosmic ray} \rightarrow C_6^{14} + n_0^1$$

The radiogenic carbon bonds with oxygen and forms carbon dioxide. The radiogenic carbon dioxide is dispersed through the atmosphere where some of

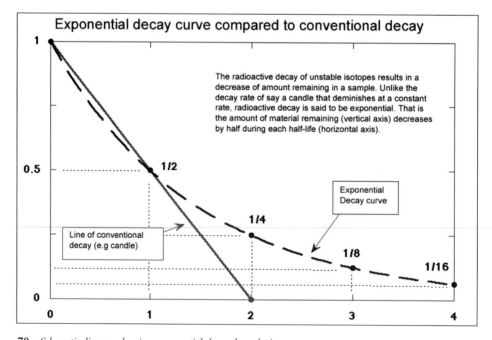

Exponential decay curve compared to conventional decay

The radioactive decay of unstable isotopes results in a decrease of amount remaining in a sample. Unlike the decay rate of say a candle that deminishes at a constant rate, radioactive decay is said to be exponential. That is the amount of material remaining (vertical axis) decreases by half during each half-life (horizontal axis).

Exponential Decay curve

Line of conventional decay (e.g candle)

70 *Schematic diagram showing exponential decay through time*

it becomes available for photosynthesis. Some is locked into sedimentary rocks through physical and chemical reactions or dissolved in bodies of water. It follows then that all living matter has incorporated into it a certain amount of radioactive carbon-14. During the lifetime of an organism, any loss of carbon-14 is topped-up through eating, so that all living matter has a base-line amount of carbon-14. Following the death of an organism, however, the natural decay of carbon-14 continues but is not replaced so that, if organic matter becomes preserved, the amount of carbon-14 it contains will be proportional to the time elapsed since death. The rate of decay is measurable and defined as a half-life, the time it takes for half of the original radioactive material to decay. After each half-life, half of the material will disappear so that, following the elapse of a further half-life, a quarter of the original material will be present, after three half-lives an eighth, and so on (**70**). This forms the basic principle behind radiocarbon age estimations of organic remains. Physicists have measured the half-life of carbon-14 to be 5,730 years give or take forty years. By measuring the amount of carbon-14 present in the material (either indirectly as a radioactive decay signal by conventional gas or scintillant counters, or directly by accelerated mass spectroscopy [AMS]) it is possible to calculate the time since death of the organic material.

Tree rings that represent annual growth can be dated precisely with no error. Such measurement of tree rings from long-lived species such as the bristle cone pine (*Pinus longeava*) that can live for several thousands of years, betrays the fact that the engine of the whole carbon-14 cycle, namely the cosmic radiation which creates the carbon-14, has been changing through time owing to all manner of factors such as solar flares and sun-spot activity, fluctuations in the earth's magnetic field, as well as major disruptions to the ratio of carbon isotopes in the so-called 'reservoir'.

Radiocarbon nomenclature
By international convention ¹⁴C years or radiocarbon years are uncalibrated age approximations, they are expressed as BP, for example, 2510±50 BP. Calibrated ages are expressed with 'cal' designation, for example, 3720 cal BC. Calibrated years are solar years not calendar years. In American publications (according to *American Antiquity* convention) ¹⁴C years or radiocarbon years are noted as BP. In Britain the convention set by the publishers of the journal *Antiquity* was followed for many years until 1998 whereby uncalibrated years were expressed bc, ad, bp, bce and calibrated dates were expressed BC, AD, BP. This caused major confusions of interpretation as by the international convention and the *Antiquity* convention the notation BP was diametrically opposed in its meaning. In the literature, therefore, there are many potential pitfalls and confusions. It is important that archaeologists publish the raw data as well as calibrated dates so that others can follow up on their data and any improvements that may be made in calibration science. Most university departments

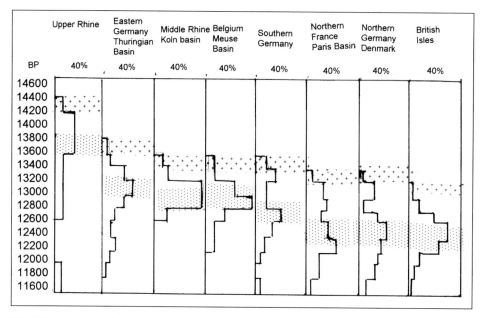

71 *The moving sum of AMS radio-carbon determinations by region.* Redrawn from Housley *et al.*, 1997

now teach and follow the international convention of BP (uncalibrated radio-carbon years) and for calibrated dates cal BC, cal AD, cal BP, or cal BCE (Before the common Era).

In 1949 Arnold and Libby produced the now–famous curve of knowns. They dated with the newly developed radiocarbon technique examples of materials from AD1400 to nearly 5,000 years old. This verified the initial assumption that radiocarbon production had been constant over the recent past and that the concentration in living things had also remained constant. Therefore, it was possible to calculate a date. However, secular variations became apparent through research into tree rings thus requiring Irish and German oaks, Douglas Fir and Sequoia plus Bristlecone pine calibration curves to correct the radiocarbon timescale.

Even the half-life determinations made by scientists vary. A half-life based offset is built into most ^{14}C time/calibrated comparisons, since conventionally expressed dates are calculated on Libby half-life of 5568±30 rather than the Cambridge half-life of 5730±40. Archaeological dates have bigger errors than calibration research because of time limitations.

Case study: agency, scientific dating techniques and chronology building

Using scientific dating techniques effectively with respect to building a past involves a critical appraisal of the 'meaning' of the date and its relation to change. For example, there is a tendency for carbon-14 dating of materials to be undertaken where the 'meaning' of the results is divorced from the crucial understanding of the theoretical implications of chronology building. This is most strongly illustrated by the notion that radiocarbon laboratories can provide a date for materials submitted. They simply do not. They provide a statistically based, probabilistically determined estimate of the time elapsed since the death of the organism that originally assimilated the carbon-14 into its tissues. The estimate assumes that all carbon-14 measured is free of contaminating sources. Radiocarbon estimates, moreover, are based on radiocarbon years that do not relate to calendar years. This is because the amount of carbon-14 assimilation into organic matter in any given year is based on the background levels of carbon-14 in the atmosphere and this amount varies from year to year. Thus a radiocarbon estimate from the laboratory is not a date but has to be converted into calibrated years through the process of calibration. It is the responsibility of the archaeologist to appreciate these aspects of carbon-14 science.

The scientific data returned from the laboratory is also meaningless archaeologically unless assimilated into the matrix of relationships that animate concepts of prehistory. What 'event' are we attempting to date? What materials are available that are likely to be associated with that event? What are the likely sources of contamination? All too often these aspects are overlooked.

If the crucial questions outlined above *are* overlooked, it is possible for so-called 'dates' to be incorrectly extended to represent other aspects of agency with respect to interpretation. For example, a radiocarbon result obtained from animal bone samples should not be automatically extended to represent cultural activity and carry with it associations of theoretical models that may be applied to the results, colonisation, for example. The extension of the meaning of scientific dating results requires that these results are explicitly theorised into archaeologically relevant interpretations.

Uncalibrated radiocarbon estimates of sample age of animal bones, ambiguously associated with human agency through the presence of 'cut marks', have been used to model waves of colonisation of people into western and northern Europe towards the end of the last ice age. This particular case study is worth discussing in some detail as it illustrates some of the advances, potentials and pitfalls of radiocarbon dating. In their paper 'Radiocarbon Evidence for the Lateglacial Human Recolonisation of Northern Europe' Housley, Gamble, Street and Pettitt examine, through the use of Accelerator Mass Spectrometry dating, the database of Lateglacial cultures involved in the recolonisation of northern Europe. Their aim was not only to determine the timing of that recolonisation, but to propose a general model of hunter-gatherer colonisation at a sub-European scale. They question how long northern Europe was abandoned by people during the last glacial episode. The processes of recolonisation are also questioned and the sequences for specific areas are outlined based on the collected carbon-14 data (127 AMS determinations and 14 conventional dates derived from cut-marked animal bone samples from eight European regions). They claim to determine a two-stage (pioneer and residential) process of recolonisation that has implications for our modelling of regional settlement patterns and the scale of Lateglacial hunting systems. They suggest recolonisation was a dynamic process, integral to, and internally driven by, the social life of Lateglacial hunters. Constraints such as environmental and resource factors are suggested but, ultimately, the recolonisation is viewed as an historical, social process similar to the adoption of farming at the onset of the Neolithic. They also claim to be able to determine rates of expansion from their data.

These archaeologists have sought to use the precision of AMS to reveal recolonisation as a process rather than an event. Through presentation of their data, they question the regional order of the initial pioneer phase, how rapid the process was and what the mechanisms of re-population were. As part of their justification, Housely et al. point out the problems with conventional C-14 dates undertaken in the 1950s and 1960s, on bone that had been poorly pre-treated to check for contaminating sources of C-14. They contrast such measurements with AMS data of cut-marked animal bone recovered from the same sites.

Since the publication of their paper, others such as Blockley, Donahue and Pollard have severely criticised the model outlined above. They point out that raw sample age estimates in uncalibrated radiocarbon years are treated as fixed dates in a timeframe. Figure **71** is based on a 'moving sum' to count the dates. Housley et al. assumed that this method would account for the standard error of the uncalibrated dates (since the bin width was chosen to be roughly the same as the average error and thus justifies treatment of the data as point estimates). The earliest occupied 'bin' on each histogram was taken to be the 'pioneer' phase and the mode of the histogram was judged to be the residential phase. A major problem with this approach, as Housely et al. point out, is that no account is taken of the two standard error required for 95 per cent confidence. Moreover, the radiocarbon estimates have become extended to represent mesolithic cultural associations and to carry with them aspects of the theoretical model of colonisation. A vast geographical model of pan-European late-glacial recolonisation is thus built on unsubstantiated data. Re-plotting the data using two standard deviations shows the model disintegrating as the phases of the model collapse into each other (**72**). The C-14 timescale does not relate to calendar years and is non-linear. Chronological relationships among dates are not known. It is therefore impossible to use uncalibrated C-14 age estimates as a linear relative chronology. The apparent chronological differences between groups of uncalibrated age estimates from the eight regions are used incorrectly to imply population movement. Another complication relates to the notorious problems of contamination associated with age estimates of bone – a material that is usually avoided or used as a corroborative measure of more reliable materials such as charcoal.

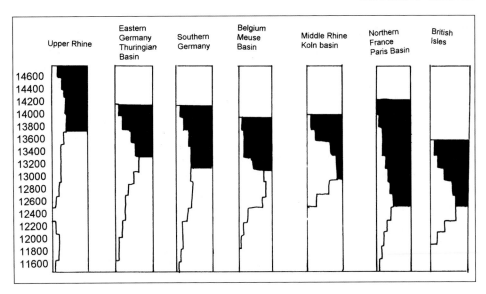

72 *Moving sum of uncalibrated dates used by Housely* et al. *(1997)* Redrawn from Blackley *et al.* (2000)

Blockley *et al.* also point out that, at only one standard deviation, and therefore only 68 per cent confidence limit, one in three of the age determinations are wrong. When the same data is presented at two standard errors, the model of population movement is difficult to sustain. The fact that the pioneer phase is defined by the earliest date also means that a single and at best just two (uncalibrated) dates are being used as the foundation of the model which is statistically unsound. When two standard errors and calibration are taken into account, there is neither evidence for a phased re-colonisation, nor identifiable pioneer and residential phases.

This case study is an important illustration of the need to appreciate the limitations of scientific dating techniques. These limitations are largely owing to misuse (such as regarding radiocarbon years as dates) or misidentification, or mis-association of samples with the target 'event', rather than systematic flaws in the technique itself.

Another brief example will serve to illustrate the problem of allowing 'dates' of materials to be extended into representations of other concepts. In North American prehistory, an area of current debate as it involves the human colonisation of the New World, there has been a tendency to regard colonisation as an event rather than a process and, moreover, one that happened earlier than first anticipated. Scientific dating techniques have been extensively used to explore the model of early colonisation. The political nature of archaeological research has also been well illustrated by this case study as land rights of Amerindians may be questioned if an early model of colonisation can be supported, especially if the players in that model are from Caucasoid (for example European) rather than mongoloid (for example Asian) racial origins.

The problem with the majority of dates so far produced involves the misidentification of sample materials. Charcoal from 'camp fires' has been revealed to be a form of coal that is naturally depleted in carbon-14 and therefore produces 'dates' that are early. Sources of organic carbon have also been misassociated with archaeological materials such as the case of an atlatl from Sloth Cave where extinct species of fauna were associated with a spear thrower of much later manufacture. To associate the bones of an extinct animal with the spear thrower and over-extend the meaning of the date to involve models of hunting and early colonisation have proved another example of archaeologists' misuse of 'dates'. When the spear thrower itself (of organic origin) was dated using AMS, the 'date' produced allowed a reinterpretation of it being a much later addition to the deposit, and not part of an early sloth hunting scenario.

Conclusions

The complexity of revealing a past in the present is daunting. Bringing many lines of evidence together from an excavation and deciding the relative importance of the materials, even finding a focus for description and discussion can be enormously frustrating. We have already explored the idea of standard views of technological and social progress being challenged by new interests and the evidence from dating that has disrupted the trusted trajectories of prehistory as played out through the ages of stone, bronze and iron. To balance this, however, there is still a need for a shorthand chronological system to allow a starting place for current debates. The shorthand chronology of stone, bronze and iron offer an enormously pixelated and distorted view of prehistory. Nevertheless, it has served the discipline for some time and allows a broad map through which archaeologists can reach their destinations and resolve some of the initial frustrations of beginning the process of revealing a past.

Placing deposits in time through dating then is just one step, albeit a crucial one, involved in archaeological interpretation. We have argued that, when scientific data relating to dating materials is over-extended to connect the elements in our field of analysis without critical appraisal, the resulting story of the past is quickly undermined. We have also argued for a critical awareness of the use of scientific dating techniques that acknowledges the theoretical primacy of investigating the technical choices made by people in the past.

7

REDEFINING THE RELATIONSHIP

Introduction

Examination of archaeological science literature published over last forty years reveals an interesting relationship between the presentation of knowledge and the developing practice of science within archaeology. In the 1960s, whilst science served archaeology with simple instrumental analyses, the literature detailed the nature and potentials of the instrumentation for the benefit of the archaeologist. From this practice emerged material specialists in the 1970s and 1980s. Literary formats were reorganised so that, rather than instrumentation being the focus, material themes dominated, aligned with technological studies of different classes of archaeological materials. It is perhaps telling that currently as archaeology re-engages with the humanness of the past and the fully social nature of technology that this book chooses to address the relationship that exists between, not archaeology and science but scientists and archaeologists. How those wielding test tubes and trowels choose to establish relationships with one another will determine the character and success of analytical endeavours in the future.

We have explored how the use of scientific analysis can be used to address a range of archaeological themes such as the use of space, specialisation, provenance and power. For each, a case study has been used to show how the analytical approaches are contingent on the archaeological question. We now develop this issue further to be explicit about how scientific analyses should be coupled with archaeological endeavours. Scientific analysis does not simply involve the characterisation of archaeological materials in scientific terms. Rather, analytical work in archaeology needs to be undertaken within a defined methodology which aims to address specific archaeological themes. A good example of this is the case study presented in chapter two where the evidence of metal-working in F630 was studied with explicit reference to specialisation and identity. Artefactual analyses were informed by a methodology which aimed to understand the use of space by undertaking high-resolution magnetic and chemical studies to map activities. Analytical work was undertaken within a methodology informed by theoretical concerns. Why have some scientists allowed themselves to continue blindly sampling and analysing outside of archaeologically meaningful questions? To gain a deeper understanding of this it is important to recognise the kinds of work scientists have commonly been involved in and, secondly, to understand the origin of our values that have allowed science to operate as it has within archaeology.

Defining analytical pedigrees

Since the first fumblings of archaeological science the mainstay of its enterprise has been the characterisation of artefacts. Such objective description of materials has been useful in inter-site and intra-site comparisons as the problems brought about by variable subjective attempts at categorisation can be avoided. Since the 1960s, scientific analyses have been supplemented by an increasing emphasis on the scientific characterisation of the technical processes responsible for artefact production along with the identification of production debris. Scientific analysis then has made a home for itself in what can be broadly classed as the study of technology. Today any archaeological study that sets out to investigate evidence for technological practice without a gamut of analytical machinery at its centre, would never be considered a 'proper' project. The reasons for the intimacy between technological studies and scientific analysis may seem self-evident but are in fact many and complex.

The application of analytical techniques has often been in the hands of scientists keen to understand the origins of their own profession. Chemists see their origin in the early pyrotechnologies of metallurgy and glass-making, whilst geologists see miners and potters as early people who first developed an understanding of the earth. Scientists have been attracted to these areas keen to establish their own professional heritage. The fact scientists were allowed to inhabit this area of archaeology is very telling. We might well ask why this area was not already sufficiently populated by archaeologists? The answer illuminates our attitudes to technology and represents what Bryan Pfaffenberger has called 'a wrong-headed view of technology'.

Technology has, until quite recently, been considered somehow outside of society. It has been considered more as a functional imperative than as a cultural product. Since it has been deemed an asocial phenomenon then it is simple to understand why it has not attracted the attention of archaeologists in greater number. They have traditionally found themselves working in explicitly 'cultural' arenas represented by ritual, mortuary and ceremonial acts. These areas have, in some way, been considered to 'represent' higher cultural practices.

Whereas technological remains are invariably hard to categorise and identify, evidence from ritual or mortuary contexts invariably associate themselves with artistic endeavours and this brings us to an important point. Archaeologists have, up until relatively recently, found themselves to be more comfortable in the domain of art which reveals the long-standing association of archaeology and art history. Archaeology, when it is seen as nothing more than art history, can hardly be considered anthropology. Further it fails to unpack or even acknowledge the cultural baggage it stands lumbered with whilst appraising the fetishised art objects of other societies. Art history works by understanding the world in terms of changing art style. Styles are seen to evolve according to their own momentum; styles unfold as though following a divinely encoded logic. Styles are seen to become exhausted or degraded once a perfect or definitive 'classical' form has been attained. What is missing in such art-historical accounts is the concept of agency or the mediated volition of those involved in the production of these works. This is a point we will return to later. The impact this has had on technological studies is clear. In the absence of material evidence that avails itself to art-historical critique, i.e. materials that are difficult to discuss in terms of style and its development, archaeologists have ignored this material thus clearing the way for this material to be dominated by scientists eager to establish the origins of their own profession.

Although scientists have an advantage over art historians in that they are usefully equipped with instruments to describe and characterise technological debris, these analyses are undertaken outside of a theorised methodology. Science is reductive and is characterised by a body of knowledge able to exclude the confusing humanness of society. Scientists have produced a rarefied account of technological history that details solely its abstract technical aspects. Such accounts are devoid of confusing social issues; stripped away are the presence of knowledgeable craftspeople replaced instead by reasonable and rational premises that assume the primacy of efficiency theory and 'common sense'. It seems scientists would have us believe after all that technology is solely practised by 'Man' driven by practical concerns but keen on conquering nature for his own benefit or profit. This image of ancient technology sounds very similar to the exploitative technologies of today stimulated as they are by the wilful desire for profit in accordance to the capitalist economy. Clearly, what is needed is a re-evaluation of how we conceptualise technology beginning with the important acknowledgement that technological production is a fully social phenomenon and hence a rich and open arena for anthropological enquiry.

The heroes of technology

The modern concept of technology has at its centre an image of determined male members trying to remove the veil of secrecy Mother Nature has cast over the world so they may benefit from their manipulation of their reality. Of course such 'exploitation' is always undertaken at a cost and this is normally the wrath of nature or the degradation of the human. The benefits of technology are of such value that these costs are worth bearing. Although such conceptions are often deemed to be relatively modern, located in the neo-classical revival of the industrialised Victorian world, they may be considered to be shared with other cultures.

Common to much European folklore is the story of the creator/craft working deity who is skilled and accomplished in production yet always suffers some form of 'humiliation' – the lamentable cost of being skilled in technological know-how. The example which best describes this is the case of Hephaistos, the Greek god of craftwork who had a special association with metal-working. The accounts of Hephaistos' birth are ambiguous but it is generally agreed that, soon after his birth, his mother Hera threw him from Olympus because of his less than perfect appearance. Through trickery involving his cunning technological inno-vations and blackmail, he won the hand of Aphrodite, goddess of Love associ-ated with copper-rich Cyprus. The union backfired in cuckoldry and his attempts at revealing Aphrodite's adultery through entangling her in a fine net that he innovated only resulted in his own humiliation. The story of Hephaistos is one of ambiguity of continued advancement and one-upmanship with attending doom and defeat. Any gain is balanced with pain and remorse. In short, the myth of the craft-working deity is a metaphor for how the Greeks understood the inception and adoption of technologies with all their benefits but in equal measure their forfeits. The inherent guilt concomitant with technolog-ical practice seems to reflect a compartmentalisation of the world. On the one hand is nature, innocence and instinct, whilst on the other reside intellect, consciousness and technology. Thus the rules which determine what technology is are the same set of rules which govern the natural world, the only difference being that they now are manipulated by the hand of man rather than the hand of the gods. The price for such arrogance is to attract the wrath of God and for humankind to begrudgingly accept the price of knowledge. It is the steady accumulation of knowledge which in turn progressively reveals the rules of nature that provides the framework by which we understand technology in terms of continual advancement and progression.

Subsequent stages of advancement, when seen in sequence, give the impres-sion technology progresses according to some internal logic as though following some predetermined evolutionary trajectory. Just like our evolving art styles with an agency all of their own, so too technology is presented in these terms. Of course what is missing is the role of the agent which, when introduced into the field of analysis, allows us to think of technologies as complex patterns of practice seamlessly woven into other social practices which offer portals for us to study specific issues relating to social relations and the circumstances surrounding the production of our material world.

How the world 'really' is

Earlier we mentioned the events that have led technological studies to be predominantly populated by the instrument wielding scientists eager to investigate the origins of their own profession. In doing so technology has been stripped bare and accounted for in only its technical aspects. As we noted earlier, this in part reflects scientists' tendencies to remove confusing human or social issues and 'stick nearer to the truth'. It is this idea of sticking nearer the truth that is worthy of further consideration.

Technological practices are not simply restricted to the technical aspects of production. We only have to think of any technological act today to realise this. Behind the production of anything, from ping-pong balls to suspension bridges, exists a legal framework, land ownership issues and the identity of the people undertaking and managing the work all of whom are affected by what they do. Introducing yourself as a ping-pong ball maker down the pub will have a very different effect than saying you are a bridge builder. Once we recognise technology is socially constituted, it becomes clear any analysis of it which renders such social factors invisible can hardly be considered to be nearer the truth.

Trying to convince scientists that the abstraction of technology to a skeletal technical pathway is an impoverished approach has proven difficult. Physical scientists have been taught that social matters are superfluous, they tend to reject these ideas out of hand. Those who do entertain the issue tend then to invoke Occam's razor, a logical principle that states one should not make more assumptions than the minimum needed. This principle is often called the *principle of parsimony* and underlies all scientific modelling and theory building. In any given model, Occam's razor helps us to 'shave off' those concepts, variables or constructs that are not really needed to explain the phenomenon. In this attempt to shave off the 'socialness' of technology scientists have in fact amputated the very object that archaeologists should be studying – human beings. Such anorexic accounts of technology should be seen as models which simply reflect the frustrations of contemporary scientists trying to deal with the social world. Clearly, the physical sciences are ill-equipped to produce satisfactory, or even 'near-truthful' accounts of technology. This tendency for scientists to produce such abstracted models on the basis they are staying closer to how the world really is has been referred to as the 'fallacy of misplaced concreteness'.

Staying near to the truth is not simply a problem of the hard scientists. Archaeologists, although keener to acknowledge the socialness of technology, have still felt more comfortable staying 'nearer to the evidence'. Perhaps the most telling evidence of this is the graphic ways in which 'the past' has been depicted. Graphic representations of ancient technology, like abstracted technical pathway models (**73**), show the reticence of archaeologists to engage fully with technological studies. Where an article on ancient technology attempts to include an image of a human engaged in technological practice they are usually desocialised, working in isolation and in deep contemplation with the task at hand (**74**). Such sanitised representations are the visual equivalent of the scientifically deduced technical pathway. In truth, both forms of representation are as fictitious as each other. In a deluded attempt to stay closer to the facts, they wander further from a presumed reality of a technology with the interwoven socialness inherently part of any human act of production. Once these important points are acknowledged, the archaeologist can feel quite liberated and begin to communicate ideas about how humans once lived their lives in much more enthralling ways. Figure **75** is an artist's representation of ironworking. It in no way purports to be a factual reconstruction of an act but can be considered a more satisfying representation or depiction of technology. The seamless integration of technological and social acts is referenced by the entwining of technological gestures with production and other gestures encountered in social life. It is a challenging piece of fiction which communicates a better understanding of ancient technology than either scientifically deduced technical pathways or indeed sanitised, isolated human shapes doing something.

Sampling of assemblages

An assemblage is a way of classifying archaeological material. David Clarke defined an assemblage as an associated set of contemporary artefact types. Obviously, the word 'contemporary' is open to debate and thus introduces fuzziness to the way we categorise. Debris like crucible fragments and slag are often referred to as a metal-working assemblage. Normally, when sampling an assemblage, analysts are keen to establish confidence in the fact that they have a representative sample. If they can be certain of this then they believe their analytical results are representative of the whole assemblage. In turn, there is the assumption the assemblage represents the process under study.

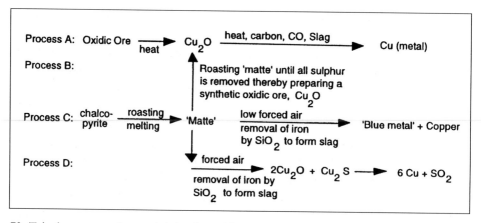

73 *Technology represented as a technical pathway.* After Moesta, 1986

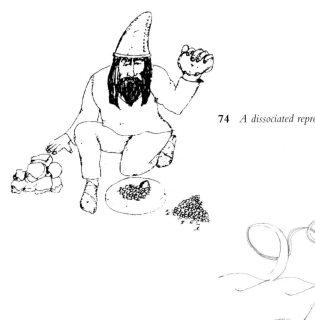

74 *A dissociated representation of technology*

75 *An artist's representation of ancient ironworking*

Sampling an assemblage involves assumptions about deposition. It is worth considering the biography of a site assemblage. Firstly there is the issue of what actually makes it into the ground. Elements from a process are deposited whilst others are recycled or even reused elsewhere. Added to this, we have issues of differential preservation that are confused by the varying abilities of archaeologists to recover material from the ground. Already our idea of taking a representative sample from an assemblage which represents a process is severely compromised.

Once the assemblage has been collated, the scientist begins to select representative samples of the whole assemblage. The assemblage most likely comes from numerous contexts, yet the scientist normally samples widely in the belief that a 'wide-ranging' sampling strategy will better represent the process to be defined. Unusual or 'funny' samples are ignored as these are deemed unrepresentative. Once in the laboratory, this representative sample of the whole assemblage is further sampled. Samples from finds such as crucibles are cut and prepared for analysis, individual finds from a site that may have been hundreds of metres wide are now analysed at the micron level but still considered representative.

Technical processes, be they ceramic production, smithing or smelting are normally discussed in terms of average compositions of raw materials and products, average temperatures of the process and average stylised forms of process architecture. Averaging results obscures the variation in an assemblage, it masks the highs and lows of analysis and adds to the confidence associated with representative samples. It creates an impression of similar results all in agreement with each other, the hallmark of a good scientist! This habit of averaging results seems at first sensible, it irons out irritating ambiguities, so-called outliers, but it most likely has its roots in the way most analysts work in industry today. Modern industrial processes are efficient because their products are valuable products and indexed on the commodity exchange. Because industrialists believe production is undertaken for the sake of profit, more efficient processes are favoured over inefficient ones. Modern industry favours the efficiency of continuous processes; a continuous process is one where production is constant, undertaken under stable conditions. For instance, in continuous aluminium production, ore is continually smelted and fed straight to a continuous casting process where it is, in turn, fed to a rolling mill. The process never stops. Central to continuous processes is the maintenance of steady state conditions stabilised by various feedback mechanisms. This makes for a consistent or uniform product – the dream of modern industrialists. This is very different to processes practised in the distant past or even two hundred years ago. In prehistory processes were neither continuous nor steady state. They took place at specific times of the year or day and would have processed batches of raw material. The conditions under which they operated probably varied hugely. The use of bag bellows would have meant a furnace atmosphere varied from being rich in oxygen to being deficient in oxygen. This point is made not to suggest an evolutionary hierarchy between batch and continuous processes but more to stress that continuous processes tend to be best represented by averaged conditions. High-quality specialist steels are made even today in the batch process because this is a better way to control certain essential properties.

Analysts working on archaeological material should try to understand the variations encountered by individuals engaged in such practices. In this light sampling becomes governed by other considerations. Averages may always be a good way of presenting analytical data but these should be accompanied by maximum and minimum values and outliers should always be reported. But this is only a small point. It is equally important to disregard the idea of a sample which, when reduced to its average, is representative. It is this single idea that has informed sampling strategy for decades and, in turn, restricted our understanding of the potential for research into ancient technologies. It is often in the extreme values or the fluctuation around an average that the evidence for human action and choice resides; both central ideas in the anthropology of technology. To accomplish such a re-orientation of technological studies it is essential to appreciate some basic points.

Firstly, there are no hard and fast rules to sampling an assemblage. Some statistically based scientists have devised rules for sampling based upon maximum inclusion size in relation to the heterogeneity of the material under examination to try and avoid these problems. Yet, in practice, analysts always try simply to take the biggest sample they can. Despite all the scientific veneer, it is still a case of the bigger the better: simple as that.

Secondly, there is the bigger issue of questioning what the archaeological material represents. The idea that archaeological evidence is somehow an accurate representation of some programmatic sequence of events acted out by automatons as if carefully following a recipe book is a very naive conception of archaeological deposits yet it appears exactly what some scientific archaeologists seem to believe! We have already questioned the idea of how archaeological evidence can be seen as a representation of 'the past', what is needed now is to see how the abandonment of this idea impacts at the very heart of our sampling methodology.

Identity, method and practice: redefining disciplinary relationships

Just as technology is not something that is 'tacked on' to society, neither should scientific analysis be tacked on to archaeological practice. It simply cannot be considered adequate that having completed an excavation, archaeologists ask scientists to analyse artefacts and other finds and to simply report in the form of an analytical catalogue. Most excavation reports show scientific analysis rendered to appendices and rarely integrated into the site synthesis. This disengagement of science and archaeological practice is rooted in the organisational structures present at the inception of their relationship. 'Hard' scientists resided in governmental and university departments with a strong sense of disciplinary purpose, whilst archaeology, a relatively new discipline, first aligned itself with art history but combined a cosmopolitan mix of amateurs and various interested academics and practitioners. What is needed is a critical reassessment of the working relationships between archaeologists and scientists, especially within the domain of technology and artefact studies.

The case studies presented in this book all share certain characteristics. They all involve scientific analysis undertaken with the aim of elucidating specific archaeological themes. Analysis was never undertaken just to add a layer of descriptive detail. Another characteristic of the case studies is the point at which scientific analysis was undertaken. Analytical potential was discussed prior to excavation and was undertaken by the person responsible for it during the excavation. Scientific analysis is much better undertaken by archaeologists versed in scientific techniques who have, at least in part, been responsible for the excavation and the recovery of samples.

Scientists enjoy wearing white coats and spending time in laboratories with peculiar pieces of instrumentation that bleep and flash. From this perspective it is easy to see why their everyday encounter with archaeology was often via a cardboard box. Bound to the laboratory bench, scientists would receive boxes from archaeologists with a note attached asking them to do some analysis more often phrased as 'Any idea what this is?' Because of this we can begin to understand why scientists have tended to study objects and production debris in isolation. Rarely do they venture into the field, and, when they do, it is quite intimidating standing alongside deft-handed trowelers who speak about soil properties and ancestor spirits in the same sentence. This absence from the field has meant they have not been able to see the relationship between the contexts from where their samples derive and hence have tended not to pay too much attention to the use of space or how process architecture might relate to technological debris. Studies which intend to address the use of space impact on scientific programmes of research at three different levels. Let us call the first the intra-contextual level and use as example a floor layer with no complex stratigraphy in a building occupied for a relatively short period. Use of space could be understood through taking soil samples at 50cm intervals and characterising them chemically and magnetically. Clearly, the scientist would have to be involved in the field to collect these samples or at least appreciate how and why they had been collected. Such studies would form an ideal basis upon which to then begin their investigation of artefacts and production debris found in association with that context.

Secondly, spatial articulation can be addressed at the inter-contextual level. Again, scientific approaches which treat an assemblage from multiple contexts as something that needs to be averaged out, miss this point. The subtle variations in debris and artefacts from related but separate contexts should be an object of study. This can provide information about contemporary practices and even go as far as to identify different strategies relating to choice and practice within an assemblage – important points when addressing issues of specialisation and identity. Too often samples from different contexts are not sampled intelligently; this is partly because it makes things more complicated and often confusing. However, such approaches have much to offer and provide an effective means by which to avoid the averaging tendencies of conventional approaches.

Lastly, there is the issue of space at the inter-site level. This can be approached in two ways. Firstly, provenance studies are ideally situated to address this issue but too often they are reported solely in terms of trade and exchange. Much more interesting would be for provenance to be understood in terms of the active consumption of artefacts and their use in constructing identity and social relations. Provenance studies also establish important details relating to the production sequence of artefacts which itself provides a powerful means by which to undertake artefact comparisons, far more powerful than simple stylistic comparison. Such an approach has been referred to as the *chaîne opératoire*, literally meaning the sequence of events associated with the production of an artefact.

The *chaîne opératoire*

The *chaîne opératoire* is a French term which relates to an ordered chain of actions, gestures and processes in the production sequence of a material or artefact. Put another way it is a way of talking about all the different actions, postures and choices associated with production and how in turn these are interwoven with social life. The *chaîne opératoire* provides a means whereby the archaeologist can infer from the spatial distribution of both macro and micro-debitage and the artefacts themselves, the procedures and choices employed by the maker. Many hold that, ultimately, it is possible to infer the conceptual template of the maker, although this is cased in controversy. If the idea of the *chaîne opératoire* is kept central to the way technological production and artefacts are studied, then we begin to see a method emerge which cannot envisage the study of an artefact in isolation. With the *chaîne opératoire* borne in mind, interesting parallels can be made with other areas of social life once the archaeologists has established the spatial articulation of activities and their associated bodily gestures. To give an example, grinding is a key operation in the smelting of metals but it is also employed in the making of bread, preparation of pigments and pottery production. If the *chaîne opératoire* of all these activities is analysed, then similarities and differences in gestures can be compared and contrasted. For instance, why is grinding of bread and clay similar but radically different for pigments and metals in a society? This draws us into questions about the identity of those involved and how this is reinforced by the gestures they employ in particular acts.

Put simply the *chaîne opératoire* is about understanding choice. Perhaps it is for these reason scientists have avoided studying technology in this way, because it does sound rather complex and messy. As Henry Kissinger once said: 'The absence of alternatives clears the mind marvellously.' Acknowledging there are more ways of bringing a specific object into existence allows us to escape from technological determinism, the idea that technology evolves by its own means. Studying the *chaîne opératoire* is an ideal way to identify in detail the subtle distinctions between objects and technological debris. It is in such studies that differences can be noted at the intra-contextual, inter-contextual and inter-site level.

Throughout this book we have stressed the role of technological choice amongst other issues such as spatial articulation with respect to investigating archaeological themes and escaping from technological deterministic arguments or interpretations that celebrate the evolving and increasing efficiencies of technologies. Archaeologists have long battled with the issue of how to understand choice, on one hand (as witnessed through agency) and the constraints of society (structure) on the other. Some scholars used to argue that the social structures determined action but where exactly do these structures reside? Of course they are imaginary concepts used by archaeologists and anthropologists to explain social phenomena. More recently, a more mature 'dialectical' understanding has emerged that sees the structures actively reproduced through social practice witnessed in agency. This realisation has engaged archaeologists in an arena of analysis where agency, time, space and material and historical contingency are key elements that are woven together to understand the nature of social relations through the construction of identity and power.

Arenas of practice

The arena of analysis referred to above brings us to the point of archaeological practice with which scientific analysis *should* be singularly engaged. Through theory and case studies we have dealt with how scientific techniques can be used to address elements of time, space, action and material contingency through choice. What is left is to come to terms with historical contingency and a clearer understanding of agency.

Agency has proven to be a rather slippery term and is often reduced to action but this is something we choose to reject. A problem that has dogged archaeologists for sometime is how to deal with agency and structure without privileging one at the expense of the other. What is needed is an appreciation of how agency negotiates deeply embedded ideological values, if you like how can agency and historical contingency be effectively integrated into a single field of analysis? Being able to examine changing practice through time, with the help of scientific dating, we are better positioned to address the issue of historical contingency and it is surely this that is the home of deeply embedded practices, the reservoir from which courses the powerful flow of tradition. As for agency then we see it not simply as action located in a single space and time but rather a concept for appreciating how actions located in time and space recreate the social relations and material reality within which the agent already finds themselves entangled. Reducing the agent to individual action forgets that agency extends beyond the corporeal reality of the individual through influential gestures and the modification of the physical and social world. Its study then allows us to address the creation and articulation of power in human societies that we would argue is the moral obligation of sociological and anthropological enquiry.

Since the end of the Second World War philosophers have debated the role of their discipline in society in light of the atrocities that were witnessed during that period of immense power differentiation in European society. From the aftermath of this catastrophe emerged an energetic and ambitious school of philosophy which aimed to make ethics its primary research concern. Even today there are clear and commonly accepted public perceptions of how the world *is* which are in a large part based on wrong-headed views of the past. The political implications of a reappraisal of science and how it is used in archaeology are important and far-reaching.

Political implications

We can summarise traditional scientific practices within archaeology as having impacted on the discipline and wider society in the following ways: technology has been rendered an asocial phenomenon beyond human control; technology is seen to evolve according to a pre-defined trajectory; technological studies are best left to scientific experts; and technological history is an account of 'man's' triumphs over nature.

In a world that has decided in its own 'mind' that it is a technological one, it can only be worrying that so many of our conceptions of technology are ill founded. We suggest this is not the result of haphazard scholarship but rather the product of certain social groups consolidating their own status and power by promulgating such ideas. The revision of the study of technology within archaeology thus finds itself, as a matter of its logical consequence, producing a radical agenda for social change and political illumination.

The rendering of technology as an asocial phenomenon has been discussed, in part, above. If technology is mistakenly believed to be beyond human control, then the effects of technological change cannot be considered to be the responsibility of any individuals or group. This is a typically nonsensical notion offered by many 'faceless' corporations where political actions undertaken to support a specific technological agenda are rendered invisible. The effects of such strategies are self-evident. If no group or individual can be seen as being responsible, to whom can any group affected by change articulate their concerns? For this reason protests organised against global corporations side step these assumptions and simply vent anger via the media. Such protests are important, not just in relation to the issues attached to the protest, but to wider academic and socio-political issues concerning human rights and corporate responsibilities. If our academic writings render technological practice beyond human control, how can humanity attend to any debate concerning it? Traditional approaches to technological study are ethically dubious and must be called into question.

Technological change has often been presented in Darwinian terms where only the fittest technologies prevail. Glimpsing at any general account of technological history will quickly show how this fitness is measured. For most general accounts it is measured in terms of efficiency, the ease at which a process can be undertaken and the efficiency with which raw materials are processed into commodities. The notions of commodity and efficiency are linked by the word profit, the single concern of true free-market capitalist economics. Traditional technological histories can be seen as legitimising the current political and economic hierarchy. If technology has always striven to improve efficiency, capitalism, with its commodification of materials, 'manpower' and energy, is the logical outcome.

Capitalism is rendered a natural phenomenon, not a questionable socio-economic construct which can be interrogated or held to account. This Myth of naturalisation has been described for the technological machinery that drives, supports and was produced by capitalism. Thus the political proximity of capitalists, economists, industrialists and traditional historians of technology is exposed.

As we mentioned at the start of this chapter, any research project aiming to study ancient technology that does not carry with it a gamut of scientific instrumentation would most likely be ridiculed. This is itself a revealing point in the politics of the history of technology. The group of scholars associated with the study of technology is self-censoring, sharing the same world view. Some areas of archaeology, notably landscape studies, have been eager to engage in a variety of approaches to practice. These areas tend not to use scientific instrumentation and are comfortable with ideas of multiple truths, plural pasts and competing theories. Not so the case for technological studies. In a disciplinary ghetto governed by scientific results and absolute values the truth is eagerly pursued, hunted down, skinned and presented by blooded scientists as their trophy to objectivity, a testament to the fact that the world is absolutely knowable. Thus the pursuit of technological data is a skilful one with hurdles to jump and specialist knowledge, only learned in practice, to be applied. For these reasons they consider it best if only specialists attend to the task. Such exclusionary tactics are eroding but not so quickly as in other areas of archaeology. In part, this is owing to some scientists believing that their work is a discipline in its own right. If indeed such a rarefied subject as archaeometallurgy is a discipline in its own right then can we presume it has no parent discipline? If so, can it not be considered by its own admission illegitimate! If technology is not studied through archaeology then all these immanent ethical issues will not dissolve but will instead endure and wreak their own social consequences, intended or otherwise.

Finally, can we really support the battle between 'Man' and Mother Nature? This enduring image of 'crafty' males pulling back the veil of myth and religion to reveal the productive fertility of Mother Nature is deeply seated in the Western capitalist mindset. Exploitation of mineral deposits and the discovery of natural laws all signify 'Man's' cunning in reaping Earth's rewards since being banished from Eden. What is most worrying about this techno-sexual metaphor is that it structures the values with which we organise our own world today. Women are still under-represented in technological practices as they are in the study of it. Further, and perhaps more worrying, is the assumptions made by many archaeologists about who did what in the past. For some inexplicable reason, it seems safe to assume metal smiths must have been male. Is this because it was too hot for women? Is it because they were scared of fire? Were they not strong enough to pick up a half-kilogram crucible? There is plenty of ethnographic evidence to suggest women are competent and capable smiths. This insistence on the masculine nature of technology, specifically metallurgy, seems to be mitigated by the unsupportable values that run right through the centre of traditional technological studies. As archaeologists and historians, we should acknowledge the ethical obligation to correct these misconceptions not for the accuracy of history but for the impact they will have on our own and future societies.

SUGGESTED READING

Barley, N., 1986, *The Innocent Anthropologist*. London

Barrett, John, 1994, *Fragments from Antiquity. An Archaeology of Social Life in Britain, 2900-1200 BC.* Oxford: Blackwell

Blockley S.P.E., Donahue R.E., Pollard A.M., 2000, Radiocarbon calibration and Late Glacial occupation in North West Europe, *Antiquity* 74, pp112-121

Bradley R., 1998, 'What do we want to know? Questions for archaeological science from the Mesolithic to the Iron Age' in J. Bayley (ed.) *Science in Archaeology: An agenda for the future*. English Heritage. 63-67

Clarke, D., 1973, Archaeology: the Loss of Innocence. *Antiquity* 47, 6-18

Craddock. P. T., 1995, *Early Metal Mining and Production*. Edinburgh

Cumberpatch C.G and Blinkhorn P.W., 1997, *Not so much a pot, more a way of life: Current approaches to artefact analysis in archaeology.* (eds) Oxbow Monograph 83: Oxbow Books.

Darvill, T., 2000, *Billown Neolithic Landscape Project, Isle of Man, 1999* (Bournemouth University School of Conservation Sciences Research Report 7). Bournemouth and Douglas: Bournemouth University and Manx National Heritage

Darvill, T., 2000, Neolithic Mann in context. In A. Ritche, (ed.) *Neolithic Orkney in its European context.* Cambridge, McDonald Institute Monographs. 371-85.

Day, P. M., Kiriatzi, E., Kilikoglou, V., 1999, Group Therapy in Crete: A Comparison Between Analyses by NAA and Thin Section Petrography of Early Minoan Pottery. *Journal of archaeological science*, Vol.26, No.8, p.1025

Dobres, M., 2000, *Technology and Social Agency: Outlining a Practice Framework for Archaeology*. Social Archaeology. Oxford: Blackwell.

Doonan R.C.P., 1999, 'Copper production in the Eastern Alps during the Bronze Age: Technological Change and the unintended Consequences of Social Reorganisation' in *Metals in Antiquity*. S. Young, A.M. Pollard, P. Budd, R. Ixer, (eds) pp72-82

Fitzpatrick, A.P., 1994, Outside in: The structure of an early Iron Age house at Dunston Park, Thatcham, Berkshire. In A.P. Fitzpatrick and E.L. Morris (eds) *The Iron Age in Wessex: Recent Work*. Salisbury: Trust for Wessex Archaeology, 68-72.

Gamble, C., 2001, *Archaeology: The Basics*. London: Routledge.

Hodder, I., 1991, *Reading the Past: Current Approaches to Interpretation in Archaeology*. Cambridge: Cambridge University Press.

Henderson J., 2001, *The Science and Archaeology of Materials*, London: Routledge.

Housley R.A, Gamble, C.S., Street, M. and Pettitt, P., 1997, Radiocarbon evidence for the Lateglacial human recolonisation of northern Europe *Proc. Prehist. Soc.* 63, 25-54.

James, S. 1999 *The Atlantic Celts: Ancient people or modern invention?* British Museum Press, London, and Madison: Univ. of Wisconsin Press.

Johnson M., 1999, *Archaeological Theory, An Introduction*, Blackwell: London.

Kassianidou, V., 1999, Bronze Age copper smelting technology in Cyprus - the evidence from Politiko Phorades. In S.M.M. Young, A.M. Pollard, P. Budd, and R.A. Ixer (eds), *Metals in Antiquity. British Archaeological Reports, International Series* 792: 91-97. Oxford: Archaeopress.

Kassianidou, V., 2001, New developments in the archaeometallurgy of Cyprus. In Y. Bassiakos, E. Aloupi, and Y. Facorellis (eds), *Archaeometry Issues in Greek Prehistory and Antiquity*, pp. 609-616.

Merkel, J., 1990, A reconstruction of copper smelting at Timna, in B Rothenberg (ed), *The Ancient Metallurgy of Copper, Researches in the Arabah, 1959-1984*, 2, 78-122. London: Institute for Archaeo-Metallurgical Studies

Pollard , M & Heron, C., 1996, Archaeological Chemistry.: Royal Society of Chemistry. Cambridge

Pollard, A and Brothwell, D, 1999, Handbook of Archaeological Sciences. Elesvier: Wiley.

Parker Pearson M. and Richards C., (eds) 1996, *Architecture and Order: Approaches to Social Space*. London: Routledge

Peacock, D.P.S., 1982, *Pottery in the Roman World: an ethnoarchaeological approach*, London

Tite, M & Sillar, B., 2000, The challenge of 'technological choices' for material science approaches in archaeology, *Archaeometry*, 42(1), 2-20

Taylor, R.E., and Aitken, M.J., eds., 1997 *Chronometric Dating in Archaeology*. New York: Plenum Press

INDEX